CELEBRATE THE GOSPEL OF JESUS

Melvin E. Banks, Sr., Litt.D.
A. Okechukwu Ogbonnaya, Ph.D.

LEADER'S GUIDE

Contributing writers:
Judith St. Clair Hull, Ph.D.
Katherine Steward
Katara Washington

Publisher
Urban Ministries, Inc.
P.O. Box 436987
Chicago, IL 60643-6987
1.800.860.8642

First Edition First Printing
ISBN: 0-940955-62-8
Catalog No. 6-5220

Copyright ©2000 by Urban Ministries, Inc. All rights reserved. No part of this publication may be reproduced, stored in a retrieval system, or transmitted in any form or by any means, electronic, mechanical, photocopy, recording, or otherwise except for brief quotations in printed reviews without prior written permission from the holder of the copyright. Scripture quotations are taken from the King James Version of the Bible unless otherwise stated. Printed in the United States of America.

TABLE OF CONTENTS

SESSION 1
Good News: Jesus Is The Messiah 10

SESSION 2
Blessed Art Thou 18

SESSION 3
Good News: Jesus Is Born 23

SESSION 4
Good News: Jesus Cares 32

SESSION 5
The Good News of Serving 40

SESSION 6
Good News: Jesus Breaks Boundaries 48

SESSION 7
Good News: Jesus Is Compassionate 56

SESSION 8
Good News: Jesus Forgives .65

SESSION 9
Jesus Is More Than Enough .74

SESSION 10
Jesus Is The Light Of the World 83

PREFACE

This Leader's Guide is designed for use with the devotional book *Celebrate the Gospel of Jesus*.

Celebrate the Gospel of Jesus is a compilation of studies dealing with lessons from the life of our Lord Jesus Christ. We are being called to celebrate the good news in the various acts performed by our Lord. For those of us who have willingly responded to the good news, we call you to celebrate the good news of His birth, the good news of His forgiveness. As we study we are being led into the rhythm of joy which may have accompanied His teaching and His action. Yes even in His announcement of His death there is cause for celebration for you to see, finally humanity can be freed from the prison of guilt and shame. What would you do if you were healed of leprosy? What would have been your response if you were there when the angels sang glory in the highest? How your heart would have leaped, if you followed Jesus through the dusty roads of Galilee and saw His compassion of the lowly and outcast. *Celebrate the Gospel of Jesus* is designed to help churches and individuals get deeper step-by-step into the life of our Lord and to lead them to celebrative joy for all that He has done.

The purpose of this Leader's Guide is to direct and assist leaders/pastors who wish to use Celebrate the Gospel of Jesus *for group Bible study. Each Bible study participant should have a copy of the book,* Celebrate the Gospel of Jesus *and the Student Workbook. Both the Leader's Guide and Student Workbook are organized in ten Bible study sessions which correspond to the ten chapters of the devotional book.*

For each session, the Leader's Guide contains:

Lesson Format and Directions for Group study directions for a two-part Bible Study lesson which can be tailored to fit the size and duration of the individual group.

Lesson Aims and Prayer Focus.

Scripture Search—questions, activities, and points for discussion of the

Scripture passage.

Chapter Highlights—selected definitions and an outline of chapter topics to facilitate review and discussion in a group setting.

Bible Study Questions and Answers—six to eight multiple part questions which allow participants to examine the Word of God and explore the biblical truths for themselves.

Personal Application Questions—three to five questions which encourage participants to evaluate their personal walk with God and challenge them to apply the Word of God in their own lives.

Church Ministry Application Questions—questions which encourage participants to incorporate biblical truth in their corporate lives as members of the local body of believers and in the ministries of their local church.

In summary, the Leader's Guide contains recommended structure, background information, related activities, and answers to the Bible Study Application questions for each session of Bible study. Due to the nature of the Life Application questions, answers for the Personal Application and Church Ministry Application questions may not be provided.

Uses. This book can be used in a variety of ways. Although this Leader's Guide is designed to facilitate group study, it can be used for both private study and family devotions, as well. Group study of the material can be conducted in private, home-study groups or within the local church setting. In the church, the Leader's Guide can be used to train teachers and deacons, and for Sunday School electives, Training Hour curriculum, adult Vacation Bible School curriculum, as well as weekday Bible studies on Christian living.

Group Study—90-Minute Session. A 90-minute group session is divided into two-parts. In Part One, participants discuss the Scripture and the corresponding chapter of the book. During Part two, the session leader divides the group into smaller groups to answer and discuss the Bible Study Application questions. The small group discussion provides each participant with an opportunity to contribute to the group's understanding and application of the material. In the final discussion, the participants reconvene with the larger group and report their findings and review the Life Applications questions.

Group Study—60-Minute Sessions. For shorter periods, only Part One of the lesson format would be used. Participants discuss the Scripture, the assigned chapter of *Celebrate the Gospel of Jesus,* and the related background information during the group meeting. If time permits, selected Bible Study Application questions can be used as a stimulus for discussion. The remaining Bible Study Application and Life Application questions might be used as a "homework" assignment or for private devotional study.

Church-Wide Retreats and Leadership Training. When all or part of a weekend is available, a study of *Celebrate the Gospel of Jesus,* can be conducted in a number of ways. For example, 10 people could be assigned to lead a workshop on a different chapter. Participants would read the entire book prior to the retreat or scheduled training. Then, they would be encouraged to select a chapter to study in depth, and then enroll in the workshop devoted to that chapter.

In the opening session, the overall leader (pastor, minister, special speaker, or lay leader) would give a presentation on the theme: *Celebrate the Gospel of Jesus* to set the tone and focus of the study. This presentation could be general (exploring historical and contemporary issues related to African American Christian living), or specific (challenging participants to examine and apply the information to the local church body).

After the opening session, participants would attend the workshops that focus on a particular chapter. These sessions should include general discussion, personal application, and produce specific suggestions and/or strategies for church ministry.

The final session would be devoted to small group discussion and reports. These reports should be given by representatives from each workshop. This final discussion would also involve sharing the answers to the Church Ministry Application section of each chapter. These suggestions may be used to plan activities for the upcoming church calendar year.

Family Devotions. Before the study of a particular chapter, each member would read the chapter privately and do the Bible Study Application questions. In devotions, the family would first discuss the chapter. Then each member could present his or her answers, opinions, and insights "round robin style." The devotion should end with personal application and prayer.

Preparing Participants for the Discussion. To prepare for the Bible study, participants should read the assigned chapter of *Celebrate the Gospel of Jesus,* before each session. Encourage participants to take time to think through the material as they read and study. Ask them to come prepared to share thoughts, Scriptures, or experiences related to information presented in the chapter. Thus, participants can contribute to the discussion—improving the depth and detail of the ideas exchanged.

Leading the Discussion. Several techniques can be used to lead group discussion. Effective leadership always requires good preparation. Begin by reading *Celebrate the Gospel of Jesus,* from beginning to end. Take noted, underline interesting or important passages, and jot down ideas which come to you.

Then survey the entire Leader's Guide. Knowing which topics will be covered, and when, will help you conduct each session more effectively. If questions come up concerning topics that will be covered in a later session, you may choose to postpone the discussion until that time. Also, feel free to tailor or modify the session to meet the needs of your group.

Before each Bible Study session:
1. Pray for wisdom.
2. Know the goal.
3. Depend of the Holy Spirit.
4. Review the material.
5. Gather any supplies or additional information you may need.

During each session:
1. Begin with prayer.
2. Maintain a relaxed, informal atmosphere.
3. Keep track of time.
4. Keep the discussion moving by asking probing questions, restating the topic, and pointing out the differences between the world's view and God's view.
5. Focus on biblical truths.
6. Encourage participants to evaluate their lifestyles, goals, and objectives and to apply the biblical truths to their own lives so that they can *Celebrate the Gospel of Jesus,* in the world today.

SESSION ONE

GOOD NEWS: JESUS IS THE MESSIAH

For sessions of 90 minutes or more, use the lesson format for PART ONE and PART TWO.

PART ONE

ACTIVITY	TIME
Introduction and Opening Prayer	5 minutes
Scripture Search	20 minutes
Chapter Highlights	15 minutes

PART TWO

ACTIVITY	TIME
Bible Study Application	20 minutes
Answers to Bible Study Application	20 minutes
Life Application Discussion	10 minutes

For sessions of less than 90 minutes, use PART ONE only and assign the Bible Study Application questions as homework.

Lesson Aims: At the end of this two-part Bible study session, the participants should be able to: a) explain the significance of the titles, "Son of Man," "Son of God," "Christ," and "Messiah"; b) describe the difference in their lives that acknowledging Christ as Lord and Saviour should make; and c) witness to others concerning who Jesus is.

Student Preparation: Adult students will profit most from these studies if they read the Scripture passage for the session and fill in the written answers as best as they can before the class begins. Then the Scripture discussion will be far more valuable, because students will have had time to meditate and think through their answers. The class may be divided into small groups of five to ten each for students to discuss their answers. This discussion will add new insights to each participant and will reinforce the things they have already discovered for themselves.

PART ONE
A. INTRODUCTION
The need to make oneself known and to be known by others is very important. Divide your class into twos and tell each pair to get to know each other. At the end of about five minutes, ask each member to introduce their partner to the class and tell what things they learned about each other. If there is time, join together in a circle and let each class member go around the room and give the name of each person until they are stumped. Give a small reward (such as a miniature candy bar) to each one who remembers everyone's name. (Adults like rewards too!) Even if class members already know one another, discuss the following questions: "Why is it important to know one another?" "What is the significance of our names?" "What is the relationship of names to their meanings in our society?" Share with your students that in most other cultures names are chosen for their meaning. In biblical days, knowing the name of a person was associated with knowing the person.

B. OPENING PRAYER
Open the session with prayer. Include the requests that God would help each participant to:
Understand what it means to call Jesus "Saviour" and "Son of God."
Receive Christ as Saviour if they have not already done so.
Worship Jesus as Saviour and Lord.

C. SCRIPTURE SEARCH
1. Begin by asking one student to read Matthew 16:13-23.
2. Ask for volunteers to read the following skit based on today's Scripture:
Jesus: Whom do people say that I, the Son of Man, am?
Disciple 1: Some say You are John the Baptist, come back to life.
Disciple 2: Some say Elijah.
Disciple 3: Some say Jeremiah.
Disciple 4: You are identified with so many prophets that I can hardly name them all.
Jesus: But who do you say that I am?
Peter: You are the Christ, the Son of the living God.
Jesus: Wonderful, Simon, son of John! You did not reach this conclusion on your own. My heavenly Father revealed that to you. We will now call you Peter, for you are a rock. I will build my church upon a rock and no

one shall destroy it. You will open the doors for the Gospel to go where it has not gone before. What you will do will have great significance for my kingdom on earth and in heaven.

Don't tell anyone that I am the Messiah. Keep it a secret for now. I have difficult days ahead. I will go through great suffering and then be killed. On the third day I will come back to life.

Peter: Oh, no, Jesus! No one will kill You!

Jesus: Do not tempt me! If you want to do what pleases God, you will not try to stop me from doing what He wants me to do.

After reading through the skit, choose new actors and challenge them to read the words in the ways that express what they think the characters were truly feeling.

D. CHAPTER HIGHLIGHTS

a. Before discussing the chapter, review the following terms:

Elias—the Greek name for Elijah

Jeremias—the Greek name for Jeremiah

Bar-jona—son of John

Christ—Greek for Messiah

elders, chief priests, scribes—Jewish religious leaders

savourest—savour means to like or take delight in

b. Using the content of Chapter One as background, give a general overview of the chapter. Be sure to include the following topics:

1. The racial identity of Jesus and its significance for both the African American community and the church as a whole.

2. The role of the Messiah from the viewpoint of Jews in Jesus' time in contrast to biblical prophecies regarding the Messiah.

3. The importance to each individual of knowing who Jesus is.

4. Peter's special place in the mission of the church.

5. Peter's misguided attempt to derail Jesus from His mission death on the Cross.

PART TWO
BIBLE STUDY APPLICATION

1. Procedure

Select small group leaders if the class is large. Choose volunteers or students who have completed writing in their answers. Plan on five to ten students per group for the best discussion. Group leaders may simply read the questions in the student workbook and let volunteers answer. Group leaders may encourage greater participation after the most assertive students give answers, by asking, "What are some other ideas?" "Who has another answer?" or even singling out a quiet person that probably has a good idea, "Cynthia, what did you write for your answer?"

B. ANSWERS TO BIBLE STUDY APPLICATION

The following answers to the questions are a guide to points that should be included.

The True Identity of Jesus (Matthew 16:13-17)

Jesus asked His followers who others thought He was; then He asked who did they say He was. As followers of Christ, we too must evaluate what we've heard about Christ and what we know about Christ. We should also evaluate who we know He is to us.

1. Look at Matthew 16:14 to see what some of Jesus' contemporaries thought regarding His identity. By this time, John the Baptist had already been beheaded. Why do you think some would say that Jesus was a reincarnation of John the Baptist? Why was this false theological reasoning?

Guide students in realizing that though reincarnation may be a popular belief, it is not biblical. Perhaps a guilty conscience or a desire to see John again led some to fear or hope he had returned from the dead. (We do not know with certainty the ideas of the people who thought Jesus was John the Baptist reincarnated, but some speculation may help us to understand the real issues.)

2. Some thought Jesus was Elijah (Elias). In Jewish families today, an extra seat and plate for Elijah are set at Passover. Look up Malachi 4:5 to see why Jews may have expected to see Elijah reappearing. See 2 Kings 2:11-12 for another reason why Elijah was expected to return. For Jesus' teaching regarding the relationship between John the Baptist and the expected return of Elijah, see Matthew 17:11-13.

Elijah was taken up into heaven without experiencing death first. For that reason and because of the prophecy in Malachi, many Jews expected to see Elijah in person again. This, however, would involve reincarnation, not a theologically true belief. John the Baptist did come in the role of an Elijah, but he was not Elijah reincarnated.

3. Jesus first identified Himself as the Son of Man. Read Daniel 7:13-14 to see the prophecy regarding this title.

The Son of Man in the Daniel passage had the appearance of a human being, but was worshiped. Though Jesus' identification of Himself is significant, even His disciples did not understand this at first.

4. What are the implications of Peter identifying Jesus as the Christ, the Son of the living God? ("Christ" is the Greek word for Messiah.)

Not only did Peter recognize Jesus as the promised Messiah, he also identified Jesus as the Son of God.

5. Read verse 17 to find out how Peter came to know the true identity of Jesus. What does this tell us regarding our own spiritual insight and our relationship with Jesus Christ?

We cannot be proud of our spiritual understanding, because even that is a blessing from God.

6. Who do you say Christ is? How have you come to realize this?

Answers will vary

Peter's Identity
(Matthew 16:18-19)

Once Peter identified Jesus as the "Christ, the Son of the living God," he was given power. This power comes only through knowing the Giver of all power.

7. "Bar-jona" means Son of John. But what does the Greek word for Peter mean? Why do you think Jesus uses the feminine form of the Greek word petra? Peter had the power to open the doors to the church for Gentile believers. Read the following verses to see how Peter used these keys to open the kingdom: Acts 2:14-41; 8:14-25; 10:34-48.

Peter or petros in the Greek means rock. The feminine form petra is used to describe the foundation of the church because Peter was to be instrumental in the building of the church.

8. How are you opening the doors of the kingdom? To whom would you like to?

Answers will vary.

The True Mission of Jesus
(Matthew 16:20-23)

Once Peter and others knew Jesus as Lord and Saviour, Christ began to share more with them, especially about His earthly mission.

Students should read Matthew 16:20-23 to see how Jesus taught His disciples the true nature of His mission and kingdom. Peter and the rest of the disciples believed Jesus was the Messiah, but Messiah as Saviour from the political domination of Rome. Although Scripture prophesied the suffering of the Messiah, all that Jews of that era could see was the glorification of the Messiah and the people of His kingdom.

9. Why do you suppose Jesus instructed His followers to keep His identity a secret? What do you think people would have done with Jesus if they heard He was the Messiah, given their ideas for the mission of the Messiah? What possible results could you expect to see because of such actions?

The crowd would have been even more anxious to crown Jesus as King, if the disciples spread this news. Jesus might have been detained from His true mission. Or Rome might have cracked down on Jesus and He would have been crucified before God's perfect time.

10. Why was it so hard for Peter to accept Jesus' teaching that He must suffer and die? How did this contradict Peter's thinking regarding the Messiah? Why was he reluctant to accept this teaching from Jesus?

Peter did not want to believe that Jesus would have to suffer for two reasons: first, he did not want to think of his dear friend suffering; and second, what Jesus said contradicted Peter's ideas of the Messiah and His kingdom. Peter wanted a powerful earthly kingdom in which all Israel's enemies would be banished and the Messiah would reign. Peter and the disciples were also thinking about exalted positions they hoped to hold in Jesus' coming kingdom (Matthew 20:20-28).

11. You might think that Jesus would accept Peter's admonition as words of care and love for Him. But Jesus rebuked Peter in very harsh terms. Why? Can we let our natural attachments get in the way of our spiritual progress? How?

Discuss how love for family members, members of the opposite sex and others can keep us from doing the will of God. One kind of love may be an exalted gift, but even Jesus instructed His followers to leave behind the love of family when it interferes with obeying Him (Luke 14:26-27).

12. The disciples heard Jesus' words on His suffering and death, but they did not understand the message about His rising again on the third day. Think of the disciples' response to news of the Resurrection. Were they inclined to believe Jesus had come back to life? Why was it so hard to believe that Jesus would suffer and die? Why was it also hard to believe the Good News of His Resurrection?

No one likes to hear that someone they love is going to suffer, but the mention of resurrection must have seemed hard to believe. However, the fact that the disciples were so resistant to believing the Resurrection makes the Resurrection easier for us to believe. The disciples had to be convinced and so the facts of the Resurrection are more convincing to us.

C. LIFE APPLICATION

Personal Application
Jesus Is My Saviour and God

These questions are designed to help students think through whether or not they have been saved, how they can witness to others regarding this salvation, and what difference acknowledging Christ as Saviour and Lord will make in their actions, words, and thoughts. You may have some in your class today who have never prayed for salvation. You may explain how to be born again or saved in the following manner: All of us have sinned, whether in big ways or small. We may think we are doing all right in comparison to others, but God's standard is perfection. He is so holy and just that He cannot tolerate sin in His presence, or anyone who has ever sinned, even in the smallest way. According to God's holy standards all sin must be punished, but because He loves us so much, He sent His Son Jesus to die on the Cross to take our punishment. So what does God want us to do? He wants us to repent of our sins. To "repent" means to turn away from our sins and turn to God. When we do this in sincere faith, God helps us to turn away from sin and put our trust in Jesus and His death on the Cross for us. God wants us to pray and tell Him that we are putting our trust in Him. Then He rolls away our sins and makes us born again or saved (whichever term you prefer both are biblically correct).

1. What difference did it make in Peter's life that he acknowledged Jesus as his Messiah and the Son of the living God? What difference will it make in ours?

2. Messiah means Saviour which means One who saves. We often talk in church about being saved or being born again. Have you ever had this kind of experience? How would you describe it? What things did you hear that helped you understand and want to be saved? How would you describe the way to be born again?

3. What differences will there be in your life when you make Jesus your Saviour and God? What are some changes in you since you have been born again? What are some additional changes that you think should take place in you?

4. How would you witness to others concerning who Jesus is? What would you tell them regarding how to be saved or born again?

Church Ministry Application
Jesus Is Our Saviour and God

Spirituality is expressed in the areas of knowledge, action, and feelings. Our belief in Jesus as Saviour and knowledge of the truths of salvation should be shared with the community in which the church is located. Does your church have a witnessing program designed to share the truths of salvation? Does your church witness through a radio or TV program? Are church visitors given packets containing tracts that explain the way of salvation? Or are teams sent out to visit their homes and share how to be born again? Are church members being trained to lead others to Christ? All of these are ways of sharing the Good News that Jesus has come as our Messiah.

The following questions will help evaluate whether your church is acknowledging Jesus as Saviour and God through verbal witnessing, through deeds that witness to the community, and through corporate effectivity that is, singing to express our trust in Jesus as Saviour and God.

1. How does a church recognize Jesus as God and Messiah?
2. A church witnesses through its teaching. Teaching is the thinking part of ministry. How is your church actively involved in teaching who Jesus is? Are you involved in this ministry?
3. A church witnesses through its people. The actions of the church as a body reveal obedience to the Lord. What church programs display a belief in Christ as Saviour and God? What is your part in this?
4. A church witnesses through its music. Choose some songs that tell of the Lordship of Christ. Choose some that emphasize that He is the Son of God. Sing some songs or hymns now as a celebration of Jesus as Messiah.

Finish class today with songs or hymns that glorify Jesus as Saviour and God.

SESSION TWO

BLESSED ART THOU

For sessions of 90 minutes or more, use the lesson format for PART ONE and PART TWO.

PART ONE

ACTIVITY	TIME
Introduction and Opening Prayer	5 minutes
Scripture Search	20 minutes
Chapter Highlights	15 minutes

PART TWO

ACTIVITY	TIME
Bible Study Application	20 minutes
Answers to Bible Study Application	20 minutes
Life Application Discussion	10 minutes

For sessions of less than 90 minutes, use PART ONE only and assign the Bible Study Application questions as homework.

Lesson Aims: At the end of this two-part Bible study session, the participants should be able to: a) describe the situation in Mary's life when Gabriel came to her; b) delight in God's grace to them; and c) desire to surrender to God's will in their own lives.

Devotional: Begin class today speculating on what Mary was doing when Gabriel appeared to her. She was all alone. Was she meditating on Scripture? Compare Hannah's song of prayer in 1 Samuel 2:1-10 with Mary's song in Luke 1:46-55. Scholars have noted similarities such as: introduction of praise and rejoicing in the Lord, God's sovereignty demonstrated in raising up the down-trodden and trampling down the rulers and the rich, God's lifting up the humble and putting down the proud, God's compassion toward the hungry, the poor, and the childless. Mary's song suggests that she spent much time meditating on God's Word. Discuss how this habit prepares us for the total submission to God's will that the Lord requires of us.

PART ONE
A. OPENING PRAYER
Open the session with prayer. Include the requests that God would help participants to:

Discover the traits in Mary that prepared her for the special calling of God.

Realize that God's blessing upon us is through His grace.

Respond by submitting ourselves to God's will.

B. SCRIPTURE SEARCH
1. Choose three readers for the roles of narrator, Gabriel, and Mary in a dramatic reading of Luke 1:26-38.

Narrator: And in the sixth month the angel Gabriel was sent from God unto a city of Galilee, named Nazareth, To a virgin espoused to a man whose name was Joseph, of the house of David; and the virgin's name was Mary. And the angel came in unto her, and said,

Gabriel: Hail, thou that art highly favoured, the Lord is with thee: blessed art thou among women.

Narrator: And when she saw him, she was troubled at his saying, and cast in her mind what manner of salutation this should be. And the angel said unto her,

Gabriel: Fear not, Mary: for thou hast found favour with God. And, behold, thou shalt conceive in thy womb, and bring forth a son, and shalt call his name JESUS. He shall be great, and shall be called the Son of the Highest: and the Lord God shall give unto him the throne of his father David. And he shall reign over the house of Jacob forever; and of his kingdom there shall be no end.

Narrator: Then said Mary unto the angel,

Mary: How shall this be, seeing I know not a man?

Narrator: And the angel answered and said unto her,

Gabriel: The Holy Ghost shall come upon thee, and the power of the Highest shall overshadow thee; therefore also that holy thing which shall be born of thee shall be called the Son of God. And, behold, thy cousin Elisabeth, she hath also conceived a son in her old age: and this is the sixth month with her, who was called barren. For with God nothing shall be impossible.

Narrator: And Mary said,
Mary: Behold the handmaiden of the Lord; be it unto me according to thy word.
Narrator: And the angel departed from her.

C. CHAPTER HIGHLIGHTS

Before discussing the chapter, review the following terms:

Espoused—This word means an engagement, but the engagements in those days were just as binding as a marriage. Written papers of divorcement were required to end the espousement. The only thing missing besides the ceremony was sexual intercourse.

Virgin—A woman who has never had intimate relations with a man.

Barren—A woman who has been physically unable to have children.

Handmaid—A servant.

Using the content of Chapter Two as background, give a general overview of the chapter. Be sure to include the following topics:

1. The social context for a young woman, such as Mary, who became pregnant before marriage.
2. The joys and sorrows of being chosen by God.
3. God's choosing men and women as a demonstration of His grace.
4. The importance of yielding to God in obedience.

PART TWO

A. BIBLE STUDY APPLICATION

1. Procedure

The questions in the student workbook are designed so students will not give simple "yes" and "no" answers. They are meant to stimulate discussion and reflection. If the students have written in their answers ahead of time, they will profit much more from this type of question. Students should have their workbooks open during the discussion.

You may choose a different discussion leader for each of the lessons. A good leader will have studied the material and written in their own answers in the student workbook. After you have directed PART ONE, the leader that has been chosen to guide the discussion will take over. This will involve reading the discussion questions and letting volunteers give their answers. Another possible procedure would be to divide the class into small discussion groups, with a designated leader for each. Coach the leaders on keeping track of the time, so that all of the questions are answered within the time allotted.

B. ANSWERS TO BIBLE STUDY APPLICATION
Mary Receives A Visit From The Angel Gabriel

Imagine that you are Mary and Gabriel approaches you. Answer the questions as if you were about to be the mother of the Saviour of the world. (*Answers will vary.*)

1. What would you say to the angel?
2. Who would be the first person you tell? Why?
3. Would you be concerned about what people would think? Explain.
4. How would you react today if God called you to do something that would cause you to lose your reputation? What spiritual resources could you call upon to obey the Lord, no matter what the cost?

Yielded Vessels

5. The Bible and our text provides us with several examples of men and women who yielded to God's will. Write a job description for a yielded servant. Use the Scriptural resumes of Mary, Paul, Martha's sister Mary, David, and other Biblical servants to compose the description. Then ask yourself if you qualify for the position of yielded servant. (*Answers will vary; check for accuracy from Scripture references.*)

Questions For God

6. Mary is not certain how she could be carrying a child. She asks Gabriel "How can this be since I have not known a man?" It's okay to ask questions, but the question is are we still able to follow God when things are not clear? Find out what the following people did when they questioned God.

   a. Abraham (Genesis 15:2, 6)—"Lord God, what wilt thou give me, seeing I go childless, and the steward of my house is this Eliezer of Damascus?" Abraham believes God although he doesn't have an heir yet.

   b. Moses (Exodus 3:11; 4:1, 29-30)—"Who am I, that I should go unto Pharoah, and that I should bring forth the children of Israel out of Egypt? Despite his questions, Moses follows God's commands and leads the children out of Egypt.

   c. Gideon (Judges 6:13; 7:15-21)—"Oh My Lord, if the Lord be with us, why then is all this befallen us? And where be all his miracles which our fathers told us of, saying, Did not the Lord bring us up from Egypt? But now the Lord hath forsaken us, and delivered us into the hands of the Midianites." Gideon proceeded to follow God's directions and successfully attached Midian.

   d. Jesus (Mark 15:34, 37)—"And at the ninth hour Jesus cried with a loud voice, saying, Eloi, Eloi, lama sabachthani? Which is, being interpreted, My God, my God, why hast thou forsaken me?" While our Saviour questioned God, He went on to fulfill His mission when He died for our sins.

C. LIFE APPLICATION DISCUSSION
Personal Application
I Submit Myself to the Lord

1. In the old devotional, "My Heart, Christ's Home," our lives are pictured as houses with a number of rooms, each room representing an area of our lives. All of us find some areas of our lives more difficult to surrender to Christ, but Jesus wants to be Lord of all. Think of the various areas that you have submitted to Christ. Now think of any areas you have not yet surrendered to Him. Pray silently or write a prayer submitting anything you have not yet surrendered to God.

Read this section aloud and allow time in silent prayer for participants to search their hearts and to surrender each area to God. You may lead in prayer: "Dear Lord, Search our hearts and show us areas that we have not yet surrendered to You. (Pause.) Help us to submit ourselves totally to You. Amen."

2. Close this section by singing, "I Have Decided to Follow Jesus."

Church Ministry Application
We Submit Our Ministry to Christ

1. Gather together with those with whom you share a ministry. Write a prayer of commitment of the ministry to Christ.

Choir members may gather with choir members, Sunday School teachers with Sunday School teachers, and so on. Choose a leader and a scribe within each group. As the leader guides the group in writing a prayer of submission to God for their ministry, the scribe will write it down. Make a copy for each member of the ministry group or post the prayer in the area in which each group regularly assembles.

2. After singing the new verse of, "I Have Decided to Follow Jesus," tell the class to take the hymn books and look for additional songs of surrender to God's will. Prayerfully sing these songs and close in prayer.

SESSION THREE

GOOD NEWS: JESUS IS BORN

For sessions of 90 minutes or more, use the lesson format for PART ONE and PART TWO.

PART ONE

ACTIVITY	TIME
Introduction and Opening Prayer	5 minutes
Scripture Search	20 minutes
Chapter Highlights	15 minutes

PART TWO

ACTIVITY	TIME
Bible Study Application	20 minutes
Life Application Discussion	15 minutes
Answers to Bible Study Application	20 minutes
Life Application	10 minutes

For sessions of less than 90 minutes, use PART ONE only and assign the Bible Study Application questions as home

Lesson Aims: At the end of this two-part Bible study session, the participants should be able to: a) describe the cultural/historical perspective from which Luke tells us of the birth of Christ; b) explain the significance of the news of the birth of Christ coming first to shepherds; and c) give personal testimonies as to the meaning of Jesus' birth for us today.

Student Preparation

Adult students will profit most from these lessons if they take the time to read through the Scriptures and answer in writing all of the questions before class begins. However, positive encouragement to do so will be of more benefit than shaming people who come to class without their assignments finished. Prior preparation will help students meditate and think through their answers. Class discussion will help them to see additional insights and will reinforce the thoughts already in their hearts and minds.

PART ONE
A. INTRODUCTION
You may introduce today's class with a discussion of the weather. "What kind of weather do we have today? How would you like to cool off today with a Christmas discussion? What you may not realize, however, is that the birth of Jesus was probably not in December. This was a date that was chosen much later by the church as a good time to celebrate His birth. And no matter what the month of Jesus' birth was, the climate of Israel is much milder than most of the United States.

B. OPENING PRAYER
Open the session with prayer. Include the requests that God would help each participant to:
- Realize anew the importance of the birth of Jesus for us today.
- Discover new insights into His birth.
- Respond by celebrating the Good News of the birth of Jesus.

C. SCRIPTURE SEARCH
1. Begin by asking one student to read Luke 2:4-20.

2. Look at maps in the back of class Bibles. Locate Galilee, Nazareth, Judaea, and Bethlehem. Look at the scale of the map and figure out how far Mary and Joseph had to travel (about 80 miles). Ask the mothers of the class to describe how they think Mary (who was nine months pregnant) felt walking on the dusty unpaved roads or riding on a smelly donkey on these same bumpy roads.

3. Reread Luke 2:8-20 silently, and then act it out. Choose one student to be the angel, several to be the heavenly host, a woman to be Mary, a man to be Joseph, and the rest may be the shepherds. Give directions for where each character should stand and then allow the angel to begin the drama. After the drama, ask the shepherds to describe how they felt when they first saw the angel. "How did you feel when you heard the angel's message? How did you want to respond when you heard the heavenly host singing praise to God?" Ask Mary and Joseph how they felt about the smelly, uncouth shepherds visiting them.

4. Ask one of the shepherds to describe the things he saw in the field, the walk to Bethlehem, and the things he saw as he entered the cave (or stable) where Jesus lay.

5. Ask several volunteers from the shepherds to tell what they said to their neighbors and family members as they returned glorifying and praising God.

D. CHAPTER HIGHLIGHTS

Before discussing the chapter, review the following terms:

Swaddling clothes—narrow strips of cloth traditionally used to wrap newborn infants to keep them warm and feeling secure as in the confines of the womb.

Manger—a feeding trough for the animals.

Espoused wife—Engagement, but in a much more binding way. No sexual intercourse was to take place, but a divorce was required to break the engagement.

Using the content of Chapter Three as background, give a general overview of the chapter. Be sure to include the following topics:

1. The historical/cultural context of Luke's account of the birth of Jesus and its significance for all people.

2. Why God would choose shepherds to be first to hear the Good News of the birth of Jesus instead of the religious and cultural elite of the day.

3. The necessity of God's reaching out to prepare our hearts to receive Him.

4. The appropriate response to God's invitation.

PART TWO
A. BIBLE STUDY APPLICATION
1. Procedure

Select small group leaders if the class is large. Choose volunteers or students who have completed writing in their answers. Plan on five to ten students per group for the best discussion. Group leaders may simply read the questions in the student workbook and let volunteers answer.

2. Individual Reflection

Question 16 asks students to record the thoughts that Mary might express in a journal concerning the day leading up to the birth of Christ through the visit of the shepherds. Encourage many students to write these journals and then publish them in a stapled booklet to help the class remember their meditations from this day.

B. LIFE APPLICATION DISCUSSION

If time permits, the larger group can then discuss the Personal Application and Church Ministry questions together.

Reassemble in the large group. Begin with a hymn or song, such as "Nobody Knows the Trouble I've Seen." Discuss the questions as a large group. Read the definition of Incarnation from a Bible dictionary after reading Hebrews 2:17-18 and Hebrews 4:15-16. Ask students to give testimonies about knowing that Jesus became a human being has helped them in their daily struggles.

Ask a volunteer to read John 1:1, 10-12, 18, 29. What has Jesus done that He could only do because He is truly God? Tell the class that if there are any present today who would like to make sure they have received and believed in Jesus and been born again, that they may stay after class today and talk with you about it.

Think through the hymns that glorify Jesus as truly God, such as "Crown Him with Many Crowns." Make a list of these songs and hymns. Do your worship services include a time when personal prayer requests are mentioned? How are these related to acknowledgment of Jesus' entering in humanity? Can this thought be more intentionally mentioned at this time of worship? Plan a liturgy that can be integrated into the worship of the church.

C. ANSWERS TO BIBLE STUDY APPLICATION
Christ Is Born (Luke 2:1-7)

These questions have some definite answers, but are designed to encourage class discussion. Encourage class members to participate.

1. Where was the King of Glory born? Read Luke 2:1-7 to discover the circumstances of the birth of Jesus. Look at the Old Testament to see the prophecy regarding the city of the birth of the Messiah. What additional information about the promised Saviour do we learn in Micah 5:2?

Not only does Micah 5:2 prophesy that the King of the Jews would be born in Bethlehem, it also tells us that this King has always existed; He is eternal.

2. In 2 Samuel 7:16, God promised that David's kingdom would be forever. How did the fact that David was the ancestor of Mary and Joseph fulfill this promise?

When Jesus, the descendent of David was born, He became the eternal King. Jesus is King forever.

3. Why did Joseph go to Bethlehem? How did the politics of the Roman empire play a part in the location of the birth of Jesus? How likely do you think it would be for the birth of Christ to be in Bethlehem just through accidental circumstances? In what other years do you think that descendants of David might be compelled to travel to Bethlehem just as their baby was due?

Joseph and Mary went to Bethlehem in response to an order from Caesar that everyone should go to the city of their ancestry to register for taxation. Thus a pagan regent unknowingly helped fulfill the prophecy of Scripture. The tribes of Israel were assigned locations more than a thousand years before the birth of Christ. They had been dispersed by various other occupying forces during this time, but they still remembered the locations of their ancestors. Seventy years after the birth of Christ, the Jews were dispersed again and they would no longer be able to go to the towns of their ancestors. Only this slim window of time would allow for the prophesied place of birth.

4. Could not our heavenly Father have found room for the birth of His Son? Why do you think Jesus was born in the stable or a cave with cows and sheep? Why was the Holy Infant laid in a manger, the feeding trough for the animals? What things can we learn regarding God's priorities in family life?

Jesus was born under very humble circumstances. The important things in a family are not wealth or comfortable circumstances. God cares about each family and is able to work in wonderful ways in each one.

Christ's Birth Is Celebrated by Angels (Luke 2:8-14)

5. What would be your response if you were invited to meet the president or some other august individual? Why? Read Luke 2:8-14 to listen to the birth announcement. (*Answers may vary.*)

6. Gabriel appeared to Mary. Now an angel appeared to the shepherds. How was the reaction of the shepherds similar to that of Mary? How did the angel try to allay the fears of the shepherds? What type of news did the angels have for the shepherds? Who was the news for?

The angel told the shepherds not to be afraid, because he was bringing good news. This news is good for all people, not just for the shepherds, or for the Jews.

7. Read the announcement in verse 11. What are the facts of the announcement? To whom was it addressed? What event was announced? Where did the event take place? What is the identification of the baby?

The event announced was the birth of Jesus. The announcement was given to "all people" of the preceding verse. The time is "today." The place was Bethlehem, the city where David was born. The Babe is the Christ (Greek for "Messiah," which is a Hebrew word), the Lord.

8. What signs did the angels give the shepherds to identify the Baby? How would these clues help the shepherds find the Baby? (Swaddling

clothes were bandage like strips wrapped around new born babies to keep them warm and to give them a womb-like secure feeling. Mangers were feeding troughs for animals.) How would shepherds be likely to be able to use these clues to find the Christ?

Shepherds, being the tenders of sheep, would know where animals of the neighboring town were housed. They would run through the city looking for a newborn baby (swaddling clothes would be a big hint for this), a unique person to find in the abode of animals.

9. What was the grand finale of the angel's announcement (v. 13)? Contrast the earthly welcome with the heavenly announcement.

Although the announcement was made to lowly shepherds, the announcement was made by a multitude of heavenly angels singing praises to God.

10. The fourteenth verse has been called the "Gloria in Excelsis Deo," the Latin words for "Glory to God in the Highest." Who is being glorified in this brief hymn by the angels?

Glory is being ascribed to God, for sending His beloved Son. The militarily enforced peace of the Roman Empire was far different from the peace that God gives. His peace is prevalent in spite of outward circumstances; His peace is in the heart.

11. The peace of earth is addressed not to everyone, but to those upon whom God's favor rests. At this time in history, there was peace throughout the Roman empire, but the peace was enforced militarily upon many occupied people. In every major city a Roman legion was stationed. How is the peace sung by the angels different from the Pax Romana (Roman Peace)?

The Pax Romana was just a cessation of military war. God offers peace within the heart regardless of the political or social situation.

12. What things do you think the shepherds would remember about this portion of the evening?

The shepherds probably remembered their shock and fear when the angel first appeared to them, the wonder they felt at the strange yet awesome message of the angel, and the unearthly beauty of the sound of the heavenly chorus.

Christ Is Visited by Shepherds (Luke 2:15-20)

13. What was the response of the shepherds to the angel's announcement? How do you think they went about finding the Baby wrapped in swaddling clothes lying in a manger?

As soon as the angels disappeared, the shepherds determined to find the Christ Child. Verse 16 tells us that they hurried. We can imagine these uncouth men running through Bethlehem at night. The city was already in an uproar with all the visitors who had come to be taxed. Maybe some people were peeking out their windows to see why men were running down the narrow streets late at night, while other people rolled over on their sleeping mats and shut their ears to this undesirable noise. The shepherds were probably shouting about a baby as they stopped by any place they knew of where animals were being housed in their attempt to find the place that was a temporary home to a newborn baby.

14. Now imagine the Nativity scene. What do you see? What sounds do you hear? What can you smell? What things do you think the shepherds will remember?

The shepherds saw a tender little baby who, in spite of the setting, was carefully wrapped in swaddling clothes, like all loved babies were in those days. Cows were mooing, while occasionally a donkey would hee haw. Chickens came to life as the shepherds were walking in on this scene. Maybe they heard the Baby crying, the mother soothing Him, and Joseph assuring Mary. The smells were familiar to shepherds farm animal smells, including straw to bed the animals, hay and other grains to feed the them.

15. Look at verses 17 and 20 to see how the shepherds responded to the heavenly Baby. What sayings do you think they will remember to tell all their friends and neighbors?

The shepherds went home praising God and telling their family members and neighbors that first an angel had appeared to them and then a heavenly chorus singing praise to God. When they tried to explain these things, they probably told how they found the Baby just as the angel had predicted. As a further attempt to understand what they had seen, they probably told people that the angels said that this Baby was a Saviour and the people probably understood that this meant Jesus was the Messiah that God had promised to send. Maybe the shepherds tried to keep track of what happened to that Baby until the holy family fled into Egypt. Maybe some of the younger of the shepherds got to hear the grown Jesus preach and teach.

16. How did Mary react to Jesus' birth? If she were writing a journal, what thoughts do you think she would might write for the events of the last two days of her life?

Begin by discussing what Mary would write in her journal and then encourage students to compose written journals that Mary might have written. (Students may have begun these for the previous lesson.)

D. LIFE APPLICATION
Personal Application
I Celebrate His Birth

The central doctrine of His birth is the Incarnation. The Incarnation means that God took up residence in human form. Jesus became fully human while fully God. His humanity was fully visible, but His glory could only be perceived by true seekers. Even His disciples were for the most part unaware of His glory while He walked with them. It is only in glimpses that people saw His Deity. The shepherds were the first outside of Mary and Joseph to see Him for who He really was. God the Son entered into a human body and experienced the weakness and dependence that we as humans experience. What difference does the birth of Jesus make in our lives?

1. Look up Hebrews 2:17-18 and Hebrews 4:15-16. In light of these Scriptures, how does the Incarnation (the Lord Jesus becoming a human being) effect you personally? Can you think of any hymns or songs that speak to the way that Jesus understands our problems because He became flesh for us?

Numerous hymns and songs focus on the topic of the humanity of Christ and its implications. See how many your students can name. "No One Understands Like Jesus" is just one.

2. Think of your present problems. How can Jesus help? Think of those temptations you are wrestling with now. How can Jesus help you? What assurance can you take from His becoming a human being?

Invite students to share with the person seated next to them how Jesus has helped them in times past.

3. The Incarnation has two sides to it "God became a human being" means that He understands our human condition. The other side is that being God, He was and is able to do what no mere human could do. Look up John 1:1, 10-12, 18, 29 to see what He is able to do for us because He is truly God and write your findings below.

Ask for a salvation testimony some class members can stand and tell how and when they were saved or born again.

4. Only a perfect person could take the punishment for our sins and die on the Cross but there is no perfect human being. We all sin. Only Jesus Christ, the Son of God, lived a perfect life, so only He can take our sins. All others would have to bare their own sins. Have you considered this part of the Incarnation? Have you called upon Jesus to take the punishment for all your sins?

Answers will vary.

Church Ministry Application
We Celebrate His Birth

1. Is the party ready to begin? Can we celebrate His birth? How does your church celebrate Jesus coming to earth as a human being? What parts of worship are geared toward an emphasis on His humanity? How does your church celebrate the Deity of Christ? What parts of worship are geared toward an emphasis on His Deity?

Discuss how worship hymns usually emphasize the deity of Christ, while personal testimonies may emphasize His humanity.

2. Plan a worship service and think about how each portion is geared to the aspect of His humanity. Think how each portion is geared to emphasize His human nature.

Plan a worship service or worship time that will be put into effect right now or within this week. Participation in planning worship may encourage fuller attendance at your Sunday morning service.

3. It is not too early to think about church worship during Advent. How can your church plan more intentionally to celebrate the birth of Jesus as both truly human and truly God?

Write down ideas your class suggests and share them with the pastor and worship minister.

SESSION FOUR

GOOD NEWS: JESUS CARES

For sessions of 90 minutes or more, use the lesson format for PART ONE and PART TWO.

PART ONE

ACTIVITY	TIME
Opening Prayer	5 minutes
Scripture Search	10 minutes
Chapter Highlights	20 minutes

PART TWO

ACTIVITY	TIME
Small Group Study	15 minutes
Large Group Presentations	25 minutes
Life Application Discussion	10 minutes
Closing Prayer	5 minutes

For sessions of less than 90 minutes, use PART ONE only and assign the Bible Study Application questions as homework.

Lesson Aims: At the end of this two-part Bible study session, the participants should be able to: a) understand how Jesus demonstrated His care for the disciples when He calmed the raging sea; b) realize how Jesus showed His care when He rescued Jairus' daughter from death; c) determine that because Jesus cares for them, they can live with peace in the midst of their storms; and d) recognize that the same power Jesus demonstrated in today's Scripture passages is available to believers today.

PART ONE
A. OPENING PRAYER

Begin class with a prayer. Include the requests that God would bless each student to:

Truly believe that Jesus cares for him/her.

Celebrate in knowing that we have the same power that Jesus used to confront our storms and other deadly situations.

Understand that because Jesus

cares, he/she can have peace in the midst of storms.

B. SCRIPTURE SEARCH
1. Ask a student to read Mark 4:37-41; 5:35-43 aloud to the group.
2. Ask volunteers to answer the following questions:
How do we know the storm in today's lesson was serious?
"And there arose a great storm of wind, and the waves beat into the ship, so that it was now full" (Mark 4:37).

What was Jesus doing on the ship?
"And he was in the hinder part of the ship, asleep on a pillow . . ." (v. 38).

How did Jesus use His power over the storm?
"And he arose, and rebuked the wind, and said unto the sea, Peace, be still. And the wind ceased, and there was a great calm" (v. 39).

What news was brought to Jairus?
". . . Thy daughter is dead: why troublest thou the Master any further?" (5:35)

What was Jesus' response to the message?
"As soon as Jesus heard the word that was spoken, he saith unto the ruler of the synagogue, Be not afraid, only believe" (v. 36).

How did Jesus raise Jairus' daughter?
"And he took the damsel by the hand, and said unto her, Talitha cumi; which is, being interpreted, Damsel, I say unto thee, arise. And straightway the damsel arose , and walked . . ." (vv. 41-42).

3. Encourage students to reflect on past storms in their lives. Ask whether or not they used Jesus' power to speak peace to their storms or did they allow the situations to engulf them. Give them time to record their answers on a separate piece of paper.

C. CHAPTER HIGHLIGHTS
As you discuss the chapter, be sure to emphasize the following points:
1. While we marvel at Jesus' power to calm the sea and raise the dead, we should not forget what He said in John 14:12: "Verily, verily, I say unto you, He that believeth on me, the works that I do shall he do also; and greater works than these shall he do; because I go unto my Father."

2. A crisis in our lives serves as an opportunity for Jesus' power to be demonstrated.

3. Our lack of trust in the Lord's power points to our unbelief.

4. The realization of Jesus' care should bring peace to our souls as we encounter storms.

5. Jesus' care also raises us from the dead and causes us to live as new creations.

PART TWO
A. BIBLE STUDY APPLICATION

1. Introduction

The Bible Study Application section contains 4 questions which provide an opportunity to examine what the Bible says about Jesus' care for us and the blessed assurance that His power is more than sufficient to handle our storms and crises. The discussion of the Bible Study Application questions should confirm that students understand how and why believers have victory despite difficult circumstances.

Allow as much time as necessary to encourage free participation and exchange of ideas and insights. Use the information preceding each set of questions to help introduce or close the discussion of a topic. Use the Bible verses to keep the discussion on track. Depending on the size and personality of the group, you can discuss as many or as few of the questions as needed.

2. Procedure

Select Small Group Leaders. Ask for volunteers or select 4 group leaders. Then assign each small group leader a number from 1- 4. (This can be done before hand to save time.) Ask the small group leaders to write their numbers on large sheets of white paper so that they can be seen from a distance.

Divide into Small Groups. Inform the participants that they will be separated into small groups. Each group will study a different set of questions and then will present their findings to the larger group at the end of the study period. The questions should be assigned as follows:

Group #1 Jesus Cares (question 1)

Group #2 Jesus Cares Enough To Handle All Crises (question 2)

Group #3 Power To Speak To Your Storm (question 3)

Group #4 Peace In Time Of Storms (question 4)

Allow Participants to Count Off by Fours. Then ask them to follow the small group leader who is holding their assigned number.

Identify the location of each group. (These locations can also be pre-printed on a sheet of paper, photocopied, and distributed to save time.) Participants should then assemble into smaller groups in their respective meeting areas.

Note: If the Bible study is small, divide into three groups and eliminate discussion group 4. You may want to include question 4 as part of the homework assignment.

B. SMALL GROUP STUDY

1. Small Group Leaders

Each group will have one topic to explore. For each topic, there is a multi-part question and related Scripture references to stimulate discussion.

2. Sharing Insights

After 15 minutes, designate someone who will summarize the small group discussion within the larger body of participants. Remind the designated person that she or he will only have five minutes to present.

C. LARGE GROUP PRESENTATIONS

Reconvene the Group. Call the small groups back together.

Explain the Procedure. Explain that a representative of each small group will share that group's reflections on the Bible Study Application questions with the larger group.

Remind Small Group Representatives of the Time. Remind each group representative that he or she should try to summarize the group's discussion in less than five minutes. Allow up to five minutes to discuss each group's presentation.

D. LIFE APPLICATION DISCUSSION*

If time permits, the larger group can then discuss the Personal Application and Church Ministry questions together.

1. Introduction

The Personal Application section contains four questions that encourage the participants to consider the teaching in light of their own lives. The Church Ministry Application section contains three questions that address some implications for the congregation as a whole.

2. Sharing Insights

This discussion should be open-ended and voluntary. The sharing of personal insights or recommendations for church ministry should be encouraged but not required. The group may have quite a bit to say. Watch the clock! Stop them after 10 minutes.

Answers are not provided for the Personal Application and Church Ministry sections because of the personal or specific nature of the questions.

E. PREPARATION FOR NEXT MEETING

Assignment. Have the participants read Chapter Five, "The Good News Of Serving" and review the questions in preparation for next week's session. Encourage them to come to the next session prepared to share their insights on the content of the chapter.

You may also want to assign small groups or particular questions to facilitate next week's meeting time.

F. CLOSING PRAYER

Hold hands, form a circle, and ask for specific prayer requests. Then ask for several volunteers to pray, keeping the prayer requests in mind.

ANSWERS TO BIBLE STUDY APPLICATION

(Suggestions for enhancing presentations are included in italics).

Jesus Cares

Sometimes when we feel overwhelmed, we may question whether anyone really cares about us and our situation. Like the disciples, we may feel like screaming out to the Lord: Don't you care if we perish?

1. The following Scriptures demonstrate the Lord's care for us. Explain each Scripture and discuss how remembering it during your storm will help you. *Encourage students to read several translations to help explain each verse.*

   a) John 1:29; John 3:16-17

   God loved the world so much that He gave us Jesus, who came to save us. Jesus cares enough to take away our sins.

   b) John 17:20-26

   Jesus cared enough to pray for all believers. He asked God to make believers united as one. Jesus told God He wanted to be with believers.

   c) 1 Peter 5:7

   The Lord wants us to cast our cares upon Him because He cares for us.

d) Psalm 139:1-10; Matthew 6:26; Luke 12:6-7

We are worth more than the birds of the air that the Lord feeds; surely He will take care of us. He even knows how many hairs we have on our heads.

Jesus Cares Enough To Handle All Crises

It's a fact. Crises will occur in life. Whether it's storms or other deadly situations, we will encounter scary and sometimes seemingly unbearable obstacles in life. When we realize that Jesus cares enough for each one of us to handle every situation, we will view our storms differently.

2. Review how Jesus handled the following crises. Discuss how the situations may relate to past or current storms in your life. *You may ask students to act out each situation and demonstrate how Jesus handled the crises.*

a) A woman had suffered from bleeding for 12 years.
(Mark 5:25-34)
When she touched Jesus, His power healed her immediately.
b) The crowd of people didn't have food to eat.
(Mark 6:34-44)
Jesus used five loaves of bread and two fish to feed more than 5,000 people.
c) The host didn't have any more wine at the wedding.
(John 2:3-10)
Jesus turned water into wine.
d) A boy was possessed by a demon.
(Luke 9:37-43)
Jesus commanded the evil spirit to come out of the boy and He healed him.
e) The widow of Nain's son had died.
(Luke 7:11-15)
Jesus commanded him to get up out of the coffin.

Power To Speak To Your Storm

In a popular contemporary gospel song, the singer belts out: "I told the storm to pass . . . storm you can't last." As Christians, we have the power to speak to our storms and other situations that attempt to take our joy.

3. Read the following Scriptures to understand more about the power we have. Discuss how the Scriptures can empower you to speak to your storm. *Have students role play stormy situations; one person can be the antagonist who tries to entice the believer to give up or become overwhelmed. The believer should*

use a listed Scripture to speak to the antagonist or "storm stirrer."

a) John 14:12

Jesus give believers His power to do greater works than He did while on earth.

b) Matthew 16:19

With the keys of the kingdom of heaven, whatever believers command on earth, will be done in heaven.

c) Matthew 7:7-8; John 14:13-14

Jesus says if we ask for anything in His name, He will grant it.

d) Acts 1:8

Jesus promises to send the Holy Spirit, which empowers believers.

e) Philippians 4:13

Because Christ strengthens us, believers can do all things.

Peace In Time Of Storms

When we realize that Jesus truly cares for us, we can have peace even when we're in the midst of a storm. Even when the winds of life are hurricane-strength and death seems imminent, we can have peace.

4. Read the following Scriptures. Match the Scripture with the reasons we should have peace. *Encourage students to think of past situations/storms when remembering each Scripture that either helped them or could have helped them.)*

Psalm 46:10	Yahweh is God.
Philippians 4:6-7	You've made your request known to God.
Isaiah 26:3	You're keeping your mind on the Lord and trusting in Him.
Romans 8:28	You love the Lord.
James 1:2-4	Your storm will bring about patience, which will make you complete.
Isaiah 54:17	You will ultimately get the victory because the weapon cannot prosper against you.
2 Corinthians 4:17-18	The storm is only temporal.

LIFE APPLICATION

Personal Application

1. A popular saying highlights three phases of life: either you're in a storm, you've just come out of a storm, or you're headed into a storm. Which phase are you in?

2. How are you handling your storm, how did you handle it, or how do you plan to handle it?

3 Think about the biggest storm you've encountered.

Who was the first person you called?

Did you speak to your storm? What did you say?

Did you question God's care?

Did you allow God to handle the storm?

Were you still peaceful in the midst of the storm?

How will you handle your next storm differently?

4. Share this lesson with someone who's going through a storm. Remind the person that the Lord cares enough to handle the storm and he/she can have peace during the situation. Encourage them to meditate on Mark 4:39, "And he arose, and rebuked the wind, and said unto the sea, Peace, be still. And the wind ceased, and there was a great calm."

Church Ministry Application

1. What storms has your church encountered? Your community?

2. How did the majority of the church congregation handle it? Were special prayer services called? Were prayer warriors summoned?

3. What programs, Bible classes, etc. can be instituted to help weather storms financial storms, spiritual storms, and physical storms?

SESSION FIVE
THE GOOD NEWS OF SERVING

For sessions of 90 minutes or more, use the lesson format for PART ONE and PART TWO.

PART ONE

ACTIVITY	TIME
Opening Prayer	5 minutes
Scripture Search	10 minutes
Chapter Highlights	20 minutes

PART TWO

ACTIVITY	TIME
Small Group Study	15 minutes
Large Group Presentations	25 minutes
Life Application Discussion	10 minutes
Closing Prayer	5 minutes

For sessions of less than 90 minutes, use PART ONE only and assign the Bible Study Application questions as homework.

Lesson Aims: By the end of this two-part Bible study session, students should: a) understand the definition of servanthood and how it relates to Christians; b) know that Jesus showed us how to be servants through His earthly ministry and His death and; c) be determined to serve God and mankind with love.

PART ONE
A. OPENING PRAYER

Begin the class with a prayer. Include the requests that God would bless students to:

Understand that every believer must assume a position of servanthood.

Realize that our love for one another identifies us as disciples of Christ.

Have the mind of Christ as they serve God and others.

B. SCRIPTURE SEARCH

1. Before you select a student to read the Scripture pas-

sages, ask students to imagine being at the Last Supper with Christ. They may select a disciple with whom they identify the most and pretend to be that person. Now have a student read John 13:1-8, 12-17, 34-35 aloud, and encourage students to think about how they'd feel as their selected disciple. You may ask them to discuss their thoughts after the reading. For a more realistic picture, you may consider washing your students' feet as the passages are read.

2. Ask students to answer the following questions:
What occasion were the disciples and Jesus celebrating?
The feast of the Passover.

What did Jesus do after they had eaten?
He laid aside his garments, poured water into a basin, washed His disciples' feet, and wiped them with a towel.

Who protested Jesus' actions and why?
Peter protested Jesus' actions because he thought it improper for the Lord to perform such a menial task.

What did Jesus tell the disciples after He had finished washing their feet?
If they are truly followers of Him, they should also wash each other's feet.

What commandment did Jesus give to the disciples?
That they love one another as Jesus loves them.
How did Jesus say people would know His disciples?
By the love they showed for one another.

C. CHAPTER HIGHLIGHTS

Using the content of Chapter Five as background, give a general overview of the chapter. Be sure to discuss the following points.
  1. Our society's attitude about servanthood point out how we feel about certain tasks and how our history of mandatory and dehumanizing servitude may affect our attitudes toward servanthood.
  2. Christ's example of servanthood discuss examples in His public ministry and His ultimate example as the Suffering Servant on the Cross.
  3. Peter's attitude toward Christ performing menial duties and how we

often think some things are too "little" or insignificant to take to the Lord.

4. The symbolism of the Passover celebration serving as the backdrop of this lesson on servanthood.

5. Jesus' command to the disciples to serve and love each other.

PART TWO
A. BIBLE STUDY APPLICATION
1. Introduction

The Bible Study Application section contains four questions which provide an opportunity to examine what the Bible says about Jesus' example of servanthood and His command to His followers to be servants and to love one another. The discussion of the Bible Study Application questions should confirm that students understand their role as servants in the family of God.

Allow as much time as necessary to encourage free participation and exchange of ideas and insights. Use the information preceding each set of questions to help introduce or close the discussion of a topic. Use the Bible verses to keep the discussion on track. Depending on the size and personality of the group, you can discuss as many or as few of the questions as needed.

2. Procedure

Select Small Group Leaders. Ask for volunteers or select four group leaders. Then assign each small group leader a number from 1- 4 (This can be done before hand to save time.) Ask the small group leaders to write their numbers on large sheets of white paper so that they can be seen from a distance.

Divide into Small Groups. Inform the participants that they will be separated into small groups. Each group will study a different set of questions and then will present their findings to the larger group at the end of the study period. The questions should be assigned as follows:

Group #1 Jesus' Teachings On Servanthood (question 1)
Group #2 Christ's Example As Suffering Servant (question 2)
Group #3 How Do We Serve One Another? (question 3)
Group #4 How Do We Love One Another? (question 4)

Allow Participants to Count Off by Fours. Then ask them to follow the small group leader who is holding their assigned number.

Identify the location of each group. (These locations can also be pre-printed on a sheet of paper, photocopied, and distributed to save time.)

Participants should then assemble into smaller groups in their respective meeting areas.

Note: If the class is small, divide into three groups and eliminate discussion group 4. You may want to include question 4 as part of the homework assignment.

B. SMALL GROUP STUDY
1. Small Group Leaders
Each group will have one topic to explore. For each topic, there is a multi-part question and related Scripture references to stimulate discussion.

2. Sharing Insights
After 15 minutes, designate someone who will summarize the small group discussion within the larger body of participants. Remind the designated person that she or he will only have five minutes to present.

C. LARGE GROUP PRESENTATIONS
Reconvene the Group. Call the small groups back together.

Explain the Procedure. Explain that a representative of each small group will share that group's reflections on the Bible Study Application questions with the larger group.

Remind Small Group Representatives of the Time. Remind each group representative that he or she should try to summarize the group's discussion in less than five minutes. Allow up to five minutes to discuss each group's presentation.

D. LIFE APPLICATION DISCUSSION*
If time permits, the larger group can then discuss the Personal Application and Church Ministry questions together.

1. Introduction
The Personal Application section contains five questions that encourage the participants to consider the teaching in light of their own lives. The Church Ministry Application section contains four questions that address some implications for the congregation as a whole.

2. Sharing Insights
This discussion should be open-ended and voluntary. The sharing of personal insights or recommendations for church ministry should be encouraged but not required. The group may have quite a bit to say. Watch the clock! Stop them after 10 minutes.

* Answers are not provided for the Personal Application and Church Ministry sections because of the personal or specific nature of the questions.

E. PREPARATION FOR NEXT MEETING

Assignment. Have the participants read Chapter Six, "Good News... Jesus Breaks Boundaries" and review the questions in preparation for next week's session. Encourage them to come to the next session prepared to share their insights on the content of the chapter.

You may also want to assign small groups or particular questions to facilitate your next meeting.

F. CLOSING PRAYER

Hold hands, form a circle, and ask for specific prayer requests. Then ask for several volunteers to pray, keeping the prayer requests in mind.

ANSWERS TO BIBLE STUDY APPLICATION

(Suggestions for enhancing presentations are included in italics).

Jesus' Teachings On Servanthood

Jesus' life is our best example on living the Christian life. Throughout His public ministry, He taught and showed His followers how to be servants.

1. Search the Scriptures to find out what Jesus said about servanthood. Match the correct Scripture with the truth it teaches. *(Encourage students to provide an example for each verse or group of verses).*

Matthew 25:14-21	Servants of the Lord who are faithful to take care of small things will be given greater things.
Matthew 20:26-27	Whoever wants to be considered great should serve his/her fellowman.
Luke 14:7-11	When you place yourself in a low position or when you are modest, you will be exalted.
Mark 4:24	The way you treat or serve others will be the way God treats or serves you.

Christ's Example As Suffering Servant

Jesus' unselfish sacrifice for our sins is the ultimate demonstration of true servanthood. By remembering the circumstances surrounding the life and death of the Messiah, we should truly live as humble servants to Him.

2. Read Isaiah 53 and write down each word or phrase that describes the suffering our Messiah endured when He came to earth to save us. *(You may suggest that the group dramatizes the "suffering" phrases from this chapter by acting out parts they've written down.)*

Verse 2—"root out of a dry ground"

Verse 3—"despised and rejected of men" "man of sorrows, and acquainted with grief" "we hid as it were our faces from him" "he was despised, and we esteemed him not"

Verse 4—"he hath borne our griefs, and carried our sorrow" "we did esteem him stricken, smitten of God, and afflicted"

Verse 5—"he was wounded for our transgressions" "bruised for our iniquities: the chastisement of our peace was upon him" "with his stripes we are healed"

Verse 6—"the Lord hath laid on him the iniquity of us all"

Verse 7—"He was oppressed, and he was afflicted, yet he opened not his mouth" "He is brought as a lamb to the slaughter, and as a sheep before her shearers is dumb, so he openeth not his mouth"

Verse 8—"He was taken from prison and from judgment" "he was cut off out of the land of the living: for the transgression of my people was he stricken"

Verse 9—"he made his grave with the wicked" "with the rich in his death"

Verse 10—"it pleased the Lord to bruise him" "he hath put him to grief"

Verse 11—"he shall bear their iniquities"

Verse 12—"poured out his soul unto death: and he was numbered with the transgressors; and he bare the sin of many"

How Do We Serve One Another?

Because we know that serving one another is a direct command from Jesus, how can we better serve the needs of others? The Bible gives us directions.

3. Fill in the blanks with the correct words. Try to answer the questions before looking up the Scripture. *(Read the same verses from several translations of the Bible.)*

a) Let nothing be done through **strife** or **vainglory;** but in lowliness of mind let each **esteem** others better than themselves. Look not every man on his **own** things, but every man also on the things of **others.** (Philippians 2:3-4)

b) Thou shall **love** the Lord thy God with all thy heart, and with all thy soul, and with all thy strength and with all thy mind; and thy **neighbour** as thyself. (Luke 10:27)

c) Now we exhort you, brethren, warn them that are unruly, **comfort** the feebleminded, **support** the weak, be **patient** toward all men. See that none render **evil** for evil unto any man; but ever follow that which is **good**, both among yourselves, and to all men. (1 Thessalonians 5:14–15)

d) Let this **mind** be in you, which was also in Christ Jesus: who, being in the form of **God**, thought it not robbery to be **equal** with God; But made himself of no reputation, and took upon him the form of a **servant**, and was made in the likeness of men. (Philippians 2:5-7)

e) We then that are strong ought to bear the infirmities of the **weak**, and not to please **ourselves**. Let every one of us please his **neighbour** for his good to edification. (Romans 15:1-2)

f) Bear ye one another's **burdens**, and so fulfil the law of **Christ**. (Galatians 6:2)

How Do We Love One Another?

Jesus told His followers to love one another. He also said our love for one another would be what distinguishes us as His followers.

4. How's your love life? Read the love chapter, 1 Corinthians 13:1-8. Find the definition for each word listed below from the love chapter. Then place it in the appropriate column. *(Use both a Bible dictionary and a thesaurus to explain the words.)*

Love (charity) does:
suffereth long (patient)
kind (caring)
rejoices in truth (happy about truth)
beareth all things (handles with patience)
hopeth all things (believes in; optimistic)
endureth all things (bears negativity/evil with patience)

Love (charity) does not:
envy (jealousy)
vaunteth (brag)
puffed up (proud/arrogant)
behave unseemly (rude)
seeketh her own (selfish)
easily provoked (angered quickly)

thinketh evil (plot; think about wrongdoings)
rejoices in iniquity (happy when evil is done)
fails (ends)

LIFE APPLICATION
Personal Application
1. How servant-minded do you consider yourself? Explain your answer.
2. What can you do to be more like Christ, a true servant?
3. How do you serve God?
4. How does God serve you?
5. Do you pray about the seemingly "little things"? Why or why not?

Rejoice in the fact that you are a child of the King and commissioned to serve mankind. Take your commission seriously.

Church Ministry Application
1. How does your church serve your community?
2. How can your church serve others more effectively?
3. Do members of your church form cliques? Are you separated by your social or economical status? Do outsiders, or people who do not look like you or act like you, feel comfortable in your church?
4. What lesson from today's session can you share with your congregation to make you more like Christ?

SESSION SIX

GOOD NEWS: JESUS BREAKS BOUNDARIES

For sessions of 90 minutes or more, use the lesson format for PART ONE and PART TWO.

PART ONE

ACTIVITY	TIME
Opening Prayer	5 minutes
Scripture Search	10 minutes
Chapter Highlights	20 minutes

PART TWO

ACTIVITY	TIME
Small Group Study	15 minutes
Large Group Presentations	25 minutes
Life Application Discussion	10 minutes
Closing Prayer	5 minutes

For sessions of less than 90 minutes, use PART ONE only and assign the Bible Study Application questions as homework.

Lesson Aims: After completing this lesson, students should know that: a) Jesus' earthly ministry broke barriers between nationality, gender, and social class; b) Jesus' death broke the barrier between sinful humans and God; and c) Jesus' Word still has the power to break barriers today.

PART ONE
A. OPENING PRAYER

Begin your session with prayer. Ask God to bless the students to:

Recognize any walls of sin in their lives that separate them from God.

Recognize the walls they have in place that separate them from others.

Embrace Christ's sacrifice and determine to live as redeemed children of God.

Realize that Christ's power can mend the wounds left from walls put up in their lives and enable them to live in unity with others.

B. SCRIPTURE SEARCH

1. Select three students to read the three parts in today's lesson passage, Matthew 8:5-13. Someone should be the narrator and read the undialogued parts, someone should read Jesus' words, and someone should read the centurion's words.

2. Ask volunteers to answer the following questions:
   a. Who approached Jesus when he entered Capernaum?
      (A centurion)
   b. What did the man want from Jesus?
      (He wanted Jesus to heal his servant.)
   c. Where was the sick man?
      (At the centurion's home)
   d. What did Jesus say when the centurion told Him that his servant was sick?
      (Jesus said he would go to the man's house and heal his servant.)
   e. What was the centurion's response to Jesus' answer?
      (He was unworthy of such a visitor as Christ; if Christ commanded a healing, it would happen.)
   f. What was Jesus' response to the centurion's faith?
      (He marveled at the centurion's faith and said He had not found such faith in Israel.)
   g. What did Jesus say would happen to many people from the east and west?
      (They would come into the kingdom with the great patriarchs.)

C. CHAPTER HIGHLIGHTS
Bible Background

Discuss the following definitions:

centurion—a commander of 100 soldiers in the Roman army. Rome was over the people of Israel, and Romans were considered as Gentiles, non-Jews.

The Boundaries of the Times—The Israelites (Jews) were God's chosen people and thought everyone else was beneath them; Jews did not associate with non-Jews, or Gentiles, who were considered unclean; entering a Gentile's home would make a Jew ceremonially unclean.

Chapter Discussion

Using the content of Chapter Six as background, give a general overview of the chapter. Be sure to include the following topics in your discussion:

1. Sin separates unholy humans from our Holy God
2. Jesus' death reconciled sinful humans to God
3. Jesus' death broke the barriers between Gentiles and Jews
4. Jesus' power can break human-made barriers today

PART TWO
A. BIBLE STUDY APPLICATION
1. Introduction

The Bible Study Application section contains six questions which provide an opportunity to examine what the Bible says about Jesus' barrier-breaking power. The discussion of the Bible Study Application questions should confirm that students understand the good news that Jesus has broken the barrier between humans and God, and His Word has the power to knock down barriers today.

Allow as much time as necessary to encourage free participation and exchange of ideas and insights. Use the information preceding each set of questions to help introduce or close the discussion of a topic. Use the Bible verses to keep the discussion on track. Depending on the size and personality of the group, you can discuss as many or as few of the questions as needed.

2. Procedure

Select Small Group Leaders. Ask for volunteers or select 4 group leaders. Then assign each small group leader a number from 1- 4 (This can be done before hand to save time.) Ask the small group leaders to write their numbers on large sheets of white paper so that they can be seen from a distance.

Divide into Small Groups. Inform the participants that they will be separated into small groups. Each group will study a different set of questions and then will present their findings to the larger group at the end of the study period. The questions should be assigned as follows:

Group #1—God Is Holy (question 1)
Group #2—Sin Separates Us From Our Holy God (questions 2-3)
Group #3—Jesus Broke The Barrier Between God And Man (question 4)
Group #4—Jesus Breaks Barriers On Earth (questions 5-6)

Allow Participants to Count Off by Fours. Then ask them to follow the small group leader who is holding their assigned number.

Identify the location of each group. (These locations can also be pre-printed on a sheet of paper, photocopied, and distributed to save time.) Participants should then assemble into smaller groups in their respective meeting areas.

Note: If the class is small, divide into three groups and eliminate one of the discussion groups. You may want to include the extra question or questions as part of the homework assignment.

B. SMALL GROUP STUDY

1. Small Group Leaders

Each group will have one topic to explore. For each topic, there is a multi-part question and related Scripture references to stimulate discussion.

2. Sharing Insights

After 15 minutes, designate someone who will summarize the small group discussion within the larger body of participants. Remind the designated person that she or he will only have five minutes to present.

C. LARGE GROUP PRESENTATIONS

Reconvene the Group. Call the small groups back together.

Explain the Procedure. Explain that a representative of each small group will share that group's reflections on the Bible Study Application questions with the larger group.

Remind Small Group Representatives of the Time. Remind each group representative that he or she should try to summarize the group's discussion in less than five minutes. Allow up to five minutes to discuss each group's presentation.

D. LIFE APPLICATION DISCUSSION*

If time permits, the larger group can then discuss the Personal Application and Church Ministry questions together.

1. Introduction

The Personal Application section contains three questions that encourage the participants to consider the teaching in light of their own lives. The Church Ministry Application section contains three questions that address some implications for the congregation as a whole.

2. Sharing Insights

This discussion should be open-ended and voluntary. The sharing of personal insights or recommendations for church ministry should be encouraged but not required. The group may have quite a bit to say. Watch the clock! Stop them after 10 minutes.

* *Answers are not provided for the Personal Application and Church Ministry* *sections because of the personal or specific nature of the questions.*

E. PREPARATION FOR NEXT MEETING

Assignment. Have the participants read Chapter Seven, "Good News: Jesus is Compassionate" and review the questions in preparation for next week's session. Encourage them to come to the next session prepared to share their insights on the content of the chapter.

You may also want to assign small groups or particular questions to facilitate your next meeting.

F. CLOSING PRAYER

Hold hands, form a circle, and ask for specific prayer requests. Then ask for several volunteers to pray, keeping the prayer requests in mind.

ANSWERS TO BIBLE STUDY APPLICATION

God Is Holy

Our God is a Holy God; recognizing His Holiness should make us understand why sin creates a barrier between us.

1. Use a concordance to find each Scripture. Then write who is speaking and why.

  a. "There is none holy as the Lord: for there is none beside thee: neither is there any rock like our God" (1 Samuel 2:2) Hannah is praising God because He blessed her with Samuel.

  b. "The Lord is righteous in all his ways, and holy in all his works" (Psalm 145:17) David is praising God for His goodness.

  c. "Who shall not fear thee, O Lord, and glorify thy name? For thou only art holy: for all nations shall come and worship before thee; for thy judgments are made manifest" (Revelation 15:4) Those who had won the victory in John's vision are praising God.

  d. "And he said, 'Draw not nigh hither: put off thy shoes from off they feet, for the place whereon thou standest is holy ground.'" (Exodus 3:5) God told Moses that He was in the presence of the Most Holy.

Sin Separates Us From Our Holy God

2. Use the Scriptures to find out what God says about sin and what it does to our relationship with our Holy God. Fill in the missing words.

  a. Behold, all souls are **mine;** as the soul of the father, so also the soul of the son is mine: the soul that **sinneth,** it shall die. (Ezekiel 18:4)

  b. For the wages of **sin** is **death;** but the gift of God is **eternal** life through

Jesus Christ our Lord. (Romans 6:23)

c. For if we **sin** wilfully after that we have received the knowledge of the **truth,** there remaineth no more sacrifice for sins . . . (Hebrews 10: 26)

d. And he that doubteth is damned if he eat, because he eateth not of **faith:** for whatsoever is not of faith is **sin.** (Romans 14:23)

e. If we say we have no **sin,** we deceive **ourselves,** and the truth is not in us. (1 John 1:9)

f. If we confess our **sins,** he is faithful and just to forgive us our sins, and to **cleanse** us from all unrighteousness. (1 John 1:9)

g. And now they **sin** more and **more,** and have made them molten images of their silver, and idols according to their own understanding, all of it the work of the craftsmen: they say of them, Let the men that sacrifice kiss the calves. (Hosea 13:2)

3. Define the sins listed in Galatians 5:19-21 and give modern-day examples. (Examples will vary)
adultery: sexually unfaithful
fornication: sex before marriage
uncleanness: unpure
lasciviousness: immorality
idolatry: worshiping someone or something other than God
witchcraft: practice of sorcery
hatred: strong anger, dislike
variance: strife
emulations: envy
wrath: strong reactions
strife: bitter conflict
seditions: inciting conflict
heresies: causing divisions
envyings: jealousy
murders: killing
drunkenness: drunk
revellings: wild parties

Jesus Broke The Barrier Between God And Man

God's design was for His people to live eternally and in harmony with our Maker. However, we let God down and sin crept onto the scene. Sin separates us from God, but He made a way for us to live with Him eternally through the sin offering of Jesus.

4. Trace the history of mankind's tumultuous relationship with God by numbering the following incidents in order of occurrence. Then find the Scripture reference(s) to describe each event.

    1. God creates the beautiful Garden of Eden for Adam to dwell in. (Genesis 2:8)
    2. God plants the tree of life and the tree of knowledge of good and evil in the garden. (Genesis 2:9)
    3. God instructs Adam to eat from all of the trees in the garden except the tree of knowledge of good and evil. (Genesis 2:16-17)
    4. Eve is created from Adam's rib. (Genesis 2:21)
    5. Satan persuades Eve to eat of the tree of knowledge of good and evil, and she persuades Adam to eat too. (Genesis 3:4-6)
    6. God curses the serpent, Adam, and Eve for their sin. (Genesis 3:14-17)
    7. Cain is marked by God for killing his brother, Abel. (Genesis 4:15)
    8. God became extremely angry with the sins of the people so he sent a flood. (Genesis 6:5-7)
    9. As the people built a tower to get to heaven, God mixed the people's languages so they could not understand each other. (Genesis 11:4-8)
    10. God promises to bless Abram. (Genesis 12:2-3)
    11. The twelve tribes of Israel are born through Jacob and Leah, Rachel, Zilphah, Bilhah.
    12. A famine brings the children of Israel to Egypt. (Genesis 47:27)
    13. The Pharoah of Egypt rejects the Israelites and makes them slaves. (Exodus 1:8-11)
    14. God sends Moses to deliver His people. (Exodus 3:9-19)
    15. The Israelites reject God and ask for a king. (1 Samuel 8:5-6)
    16. God promises to tear apart the united kingdom of Israel because of Solomon's insistence on worshiping idols. (1 Kings 11:11)
    17. The Messiah is born. (Matthew 2:1)
    18. Jesus dies and the curtain in the Temple is torn. (Matthew 27:50-51)
    19. Jesus conquerors death. (Matthew 28:5-6)

Jesus Breaks Barriers On Earth

5. Discuss the barriers set up in the following situations, and write down what Jesus said to the people to break the barriers.

    a. The Samaritan woman at the well (John 4:13): The barriers were that she was a non-Jew and a woman. "Whosoever drinketh of this water shall thirst again: But whosoever drinketh of the water that I shall give him shall never thirst; but the water that I shall give him shall be in him a well of water springing up into everlasting life."

    b. The Gentile mother (Mark 7:29): The barrier was that she was a non-Jew. "For this saying go thy way; the devil is gone out of thy daughter."

    c. The woman caught in adultery (John 8:11): The barriers were that she had broken the law and was a woman."Neither do I condemn thee; go, and sin no more."

    d. The man with a crippled hand (Mark 3:1-5): The barrier was the law, which made it unlawful to heal on the Sabbath. "Stretch forth thy hand."

6. The following Scriptures tell us what God says about barriers. Match the Scripture with the barrier.

James 2:2-9	Do not show favoritism for the rich and well-dressed.
Hebrews 13:3	Show compassion toward prisoners.
Matthew 28:19	Teach all nations.
John 3:16	Whoever believes in God's Son shall have everlasting life.
Galatians 3:28	Everyone, regardless of nationality, gender, or position is the same in Christ.

LIFE APPLICATION
Personal Application

    1. What sins separate you from God? Confess your sins and be cleansed.

    2. What barriers do you have between others who are of a different race, gender, socio-economic group, etc.?

    3. How can you break down those barriers?

Church Ministry Application

    1. What barriers does your church have up between different races, genders, or socio-economic groups?

    2. What programs can be instituted to help break down some barriers?

    3. Who's suffering in your community? What can be done to help them and how?

SESSION SEVEN

GOOD NEWS: JESUS IS COMPASSIONATE

For sessions of 90 minutes or more, use the lesson format for PART ONE and PART TWO.

PART ONE

ACTIVITY	TIME
Opening Prayer	5 minutes
Scripture Search	15 minutes
Chapter Highlights	15 minutes

PART TWO

ACTIVITY	TIME
Small Group Study	15 minutes
Large Group Presentations	20 minutes
Life Application Discussion	15 minutes
Closing Prayer	5 minutes

For sessions of less than 90 minutes, use PART ONE only and assign the Bible Study Application questions as homework.

Lesson Aims: By the end of the lesson, students will be able to: a) recount some of Jesus' acts of compassion; b) understand that God is compassionate and suffers when we suffer; and c) will determine to become more compassionate towards others in need.

PART ONE
A. OPENING PRAYER

Open the session with prayer. Include the requests that God would help each participant to:

Realize that God feels pain we suffer.

Be thankful to God for being merciful and compassionate.

Choose to open their hearts, change their attitudes, and be more compassionate towards others.

B. SCRIPTURE SEARCH

1. Ask someone to read Mark 7:32-37 aloud to the group.

2. Use the following questions to review the facts from this Scripture passage:

a) What was the condition of the man brought to Jesus? (7:32)
The man brought to Jesus was deaf and he had a speech impediment.
b) What did Jesus do to the man? What was the result? (vv. 33-35)
Jesus put His finger into the man's ear, spit, looked up to heaven, and ordered the man's ears to be opened. Immediately, they opened, the man's tongue was loosed and he was able to speak clearly.
c) What was the response of those who witnessed this miracle? (vv. 36-37)
Those who witnessed this miracle were amazed. Jesus instructed them not to tell anyone what they saw, but the men could not contain themselves. They made a big deal of it, telling all they could.

3. Ask another volunteer to read Mark 10:46-52 aloud to the group.
4. Use the following questions to review the facts from this Scripture passage:

a.) What was Bartimaeus' impediment? (verse 46)
Bartimaeus was blind.
b.) What was Bartimaeus' response when he heard that Jesus was there in Jericho? (vv. 47-48)
Bartimaeus called out to Jesus pleading for Him to have mercy on him. Though many said Bartimaeus should be quiet, he continued crying out to Jesus for mercy.
c.) What was Jesus' response to Bartimaeus? (vv. 49-52)
Jesus called Bartimaeus and asked him what he desired. Bartimaeus asked Jesus for his eyesight, which Jesus immediately gave to him.
d.) What, according to Jesus, allowed Bartimaeus to receive his sight? (v. 52)

5. Ask the group to define the word "compassion." Allow a few minutes for volunteer response. Compassion is defined in the dictionary as "the feeling of sharing the suffering of another, together with a desire to give aid or to show mercy." Note the phrase, "sharing the suffering of another." Jesus suffered for us all when He died on the cross (Luke 9:22). With that in mind, why, then, must we as Christians suffer?

- Use the following points to discuss human suffering:
- Is not always because of sin (John 9:2-3)
- Tests our faith (James 1:3)
- Allows us to call on God and cast our burdens on Him (Psalm 55:22; Psalm 88:9)

- Allows God to comfort us (2 Corinthians 1:4)
- Allows God to be involved in our troubles (2 Corinthians 1:57)
- Builds patience and endurance (2 Corinthians 1:6)

6. Finally, point out to the group that suffering challenges us to show compassion to others. How do we respond to those who are suffering? Do we show compassion? Is it our duty to show compassion?

7. End the discussion by asking a volunteer to read 1 Peter 3:8-17 aloud to the group.

C. CHAPTER HIGHLIGHTS

Using the content of Chapter Seven as background, give a general overview of the chapter. Be sure to include the following topics:

1. Jesus' Compassion Towards Us
2. Our Compassion Towards Others

PART TWO
A. BIBLE STUDY APPLICATION
1. Introduction

The Bible Study Application section contains nine questions which provide an opportunity to understand more fully the meaning of compassion. The discussion of the Bible Study Application questions should confirm that the students understand the importance of Scripture.

Allow as much time as necessary to encourage the exchange of ideas and insights. Use the information preceding each set of questions to help introduce or close the discussion of a topic. Use the Bible verses to help keep the discussion on track. Depending on the size and personality of the group, you can discuss as many or as few of the questions as needed.

2. Procedure

Select Small Group Leaders. Ask for volunteers or select two small group leaders.

Divide into Two Groups. Inform the participants that they will be separated into small groups. Each group will study a different set of questions and then will present their findings to the larger group at the end of the study period. The questions should be assigned as follows:

Group #1: Jesus' Compassion Towards Us (Questions #1-5)
Group #2: Our Compassion Towards Others (Questions #6-9)

B. SMALL GROUP STUDY

1. Small Group Leaders

Each group will have one topic to explore. For each topic, there are questions and related Scripture references to stimulate discussion.

2. Sharing Insights

After 15 minutes, designate someone who will summarize the small group within the larger body of participants. Remind the designated person that she or he will only have ten minutes to present.

C. LARGE GROUP PRESENTATIONS

Reconvene the Group. Call the small groups back together.

Explain the Procedure. Explain that a representative of each small group will share that group's reflections on the Bible Study Application questions with the larger group.

Remind Small Group Representatives of the time. Remind each group representative that he or she should try to summarize the group's discussion in ten minutes. Allow up to five minutes to discuss each group's presentation.

D. LIFE APPLICATION DISCUSSION*

If time permits, the larger group can then discuss the Personal Application and Church Ministry questions together.

1. Introduction

The Personal Application sections contains three questions that encourage the participants to consider the teaching in light of their own lives. The Church Ministry Application section contains two questions which address some implications for the congregation as a whole.

2. Sharing Insights

This discussion should be open-ended and voluntary. The sharing of personal insights or recommendations for church ministry should be encouraged but not required. The group may have quite a bit to say. Watch the clock! Stop them after 10 minutes.

*Answers are not provided for the Personal Application and Church Ministry sections because of the personal or specific nature of the questions.

E. PREPARATION FOR NEXT MEETING

Assignment. Have the participants read Chapter Eight, "Good News: Jesus Forgives" and review the questions in preparation for next week's session. Encourage them to come to the next session prepared to share their insights on the content of the chapter.

In addition, assign each person the following: Give each member of the group a chain link made from construction paper. Challenge each member to perform an act of compassion this week, and document that act on their link. Have everyone return their chain link next week and link all of the acts of compassion together to form a compassion chain. Continue to add on to the each week, knowing that each added link is helping to build a more compassionate church body.

F. CLOSING PRAYER

Form a circle, hold hands and ask for specific prayer requests. Then ask for several volunteers to pray, keeping the prayer requests in mind.

ANSWERS TO BIBLE STUDY APPLICATION

Jesus' Compassion Towards Us

"Everything he does is wonderful; he even corrects deafness and stammering" (Mark 7:37, LB).

1. Look up Mark 7:32 and write it below.

"And they bring unto him one that was deaf, and had an impediment in his speech; and they beseech him to put his hand upon him."

a. Why was the deaf man brought to Jesus by someone in the crowd?

Someone in the crowd was sensitive to the deaf man's plight and knew he needed to see Jesus. This suggests that the person who brought the deaf man to Jesus had faith and knew that Jesus could heal any illness, including deafness and speech impediments.

b. The man in the above question physically brought the deaf man to Jesus. How can we bring someone to Jesus?

We can bring someone to Jesus through prayer. (Colossians 1:9)

c. Find Mark 7:34. Write it below.

"And looking up to heaven, he sighed, and saith unto him, Ephphatha, that is, Be opened."

d. What does this verse tell us about Jesus' relationship with the Father?

Jesus wanted to constantly stay in touch with the Father. He did not want to depend on His own strength, but draw His strength from the Father. It is suggestive of how our relationship with the Father should be.

2. Read Mark 15:21. Could Jesus have saved Himself? Explain how Jesus' act showed the ultimate compassion for us.

Yes, Jesus could have saved Himself — He is Christ the King! He could have come down from the cross and refused to endure the physical torture and separation from God. Jesus did not come down because He loves us. He was willing to endure our suffering, bear our pain, and pay the price for our sins so we could be restored with God. His compassion was so great, not only was He dying for us, He was dying for those who were killing Him.

3. On the lines below, tell how Jesus showed compassion in the following Scriptures.

a. Mark 1:40-42

A man with leprosy came to Jesus and asked to be made clean. Jesus was filled with compassion, touched the man and he was immediately healed of his leprosy.

b. Mark 8:1-9

Jesus felt compassion for a crowd of 4000 who had nothing to eat. Jesus took a few small fish and seven loaves of bread and fed everyone present. Not only were they fed, they were full (satisfied).

4. The following Scriptures from Psalms speak of God's compassion. Unscramble each word in bold to correctly complete the Scripture.

Psalm 78:38

But he, being full of compassion, forgave their **INIQUITY**, and destroyed them not: yea, many a time turned he his **ANGER** away, and did not stir up all his **WRATH**.

Psalm 86:15

But thou, O Lord, art a God full of compassion, and **GRACIOUS, LONG-SUFFERING,** and **PLENTEOUS** in mercy and truth.

Psalm 111:4

He hath made his wonderful **WORKS** to be **REMEMBERED**: the Lord is gracious and **FULL** of compassion.

Psalm 112:4

Unto the **UPRIGHT** there ariseth light in the **DARKNESS**: he is gracious, and full of compassion, and **RIGHTEOUS**.

Psalm 145:8
The **LORD** is gracious, and full of compassion; **SLOW** to anger, and of great **MERCY**.

5. The following events took place in Mark 10:46-52. Can you put them in the correct order of occurrence?
    4 Jesus asked Bartimaeus wanted he wanted Jesus to do.
    3 The people suggested Bartimaeus hold his peace.
    1 Bartimaeus sat beside the highway and begged.
    6 Jesus told Bartimaeus to go; his faith healed him.
    2 Bartimaeus cried out for mercy.
    5 Bartimaeus asked for his sight.

Our Compassion Towards Others
Jesus went about doing good. Those of us who would be His followers are challenged by Him to show compassion to others as He has shown it to us.

6. Prayer is one way to show compassion for another. Read Colossians 1:9-11. List some of the things that you can pray for another person.
You can pray:
- That God helps them to know His will
- That God will give them wisdom and spiritual understanding
- That they live a life pleasing to the Lord
- That they are given strength, endurance, patience and joy

7. Read the following Scriptures. Complete each one by using a word from the Word Bank.
a. Mark 7:37
And were beyond measure **astonished,** saying, He hath done all things well: he maketh both the deaf to hear, and the dumb to speak.
b. Matthew 18:33
Shouldest not thou also have had compassion on thy fellowservant, even as I had **pity** on thee?
c. Luke 10:33
But a certain **Samaritan,** as he journeyed, came where he was: and when he saw him, he had compassion on him
d. Hebrews 5:2
Who can have compassion on the **ignorant**, and on them that are out of the way; for that he himself also is compassed with infirmity.

e. 1 Peter 3:8
Finally, be ye all of one mind, having compassion one of another, **love** as brethren, be pitiful, be courteous:

f. 1 John 3:17
But whoso hath this world's good, and seeth his brother have need, and shutteth up his **bowels** of compassion from him, how dwelleth the love of God in him?

g. Jude 1:22
And of some have compassion, making a **difference**

8. Read John 8:3-7. Answer the following questions.
a. Why was the crowd going to stone the woman? (v. 3)
They were going to stone her because she was an adulterer.
b. What challenge did Jesus issue to the crowd? (v.7)
Jesus said the one among them without sin should throw the first stone.
c. What does this passage tell us about extending compassion to others?
Answers will vary. It is important that we not judge others but be merciful and full of compassion knowing that our God is both merciful and full of compassion. Unless we are *the exception*, one without sin, then we are in as much need for God's compassion and mercy as the next person.

9. What is our obligation to others? Look up the following Scriptures and write them below.

Luke 6:37-38
Judge not, and ye shall not be judged: condemn not, and ye shall not be condemned: forgive, and ye shall be forgiven: 38 Give, and it shall be given unto you; good measure, pressed down, and shaken together, and running over, shall men give into your bosom. For with the same measure that ye mete withal it shall be measured to you again.

Obadiah 1:12, 15
But thou shouldest not have looked on the day of thy brother in the day that he became a stranger; neither shouldest thou have rejoiced over the children of Judah in the day of their destruction; neither shouldest thou have spoken proudly in the day of distress. 15 For the day of the Lord is near upon all the heathen: as thou hast done, it shall be done unto thee: thy reward shall return upon thine own head.

Galatians 4:13-14
Ye know how through infirmity of the flesh I preached the gospel unto you at the first. 14 And my temptation which was in my flesh ye despised

not, nor rejected; but received me as an angel of God, even as Christ Jesus.

Romans 13:8-10

Owe no man any thing, but to love one another: for he that loveth another hath fulfilled the law. 9 For this, Thou shalt not commit adultery, Thou shalt not kill, Thou shalt not steal, Thou shalt not bear false witness, Thou shalt not covet; and if there be any other commandment, it is briefly comprehended in this saying, namely, Thou shalt love thy neighbour as thyself. 10 Love worketh no ill to his neighbour: therefore love is the fulfilling of the law.

LIFE APPLICATION

Personal Application

1. Have you ever felt frustrated or impatient when trying to help another deal with a problem? What can you do in the future to avoid such feelings?

2. Read Mark 6:34. How can you apply this Scripture to your own life?

3. What is the difference between compassion and pity? Can they affect the way you deal with others?

Church Ministry Application

1. To what extent is the church responsible for reaching out to members who are suffering? Does this responsibility extend beyond the church?

2. Why is there so much suffering in the world today? How can the church help people gain a balanced perspective, knowing that though there is much suffering, there is also much joy?

SESSION EIGHT

GOOD NEWS: JESUS FORGIVES

For sessions of 90 minutes or more, use the lesson format for PART ONE and PART TWO.

PART ONE

ACTIVITY	TIME
Opening Prayer	5 minutes
Scripture Search	15 minutes
Chapter Highlights	15 minutes

PART TWO

ACTIVITY	TIME
Small Group Study	15 minutes
Large Group Presentations	27 minutes
Large Group Discussion	10 minutes
Closing Prayer	3 minutes

For sessions of less than 90 minutes, use PART ONE only and assign the Bible Study Application questions as home

Lesson Aims: By the end of the lesson, students will be able to: a) accurately retell the parable of the unforgiving servant; b) have a deeper understanding of the meaning and importance of forgiveness and; c) recognize the importance of accepting God's forgiveness and extending forgiveness to others.

PART ONE
A. OPENING PRAYER

Open the session with prayer. Include the requests that God would help each participant to:

Truly understand the meaning and necessity of forgiveness.

Accept God's gift of forgiveness and be repentant for ones sins.

Choose to extend forgiveness to others indiscriminately and completely.

B. SCRIPTURE SEARCH

1. Ask someone to read Matthew 18:21-35 aloud to the group.

2. Use the following questions

to review the facts from this Scripture passage:

a) According to Jesus, at least how often should we forgive our brothers and sisters? What does that mean? (v. 22)

Jesus said we should forgive at least seventy times seven. This implies that there should be no limit placed on the amount of times forgiveness is extended to another.

b) To what did Jesus compare the kingdom of heaven? (v. 23)

Jesus compared the kingdom of heaven to a king who is trying to settle the accounts of his servants.

c) How did the king handle the servant who owed ten thousand talents but could not repay them? (vv. 25-27)

The servant pleaded for patience and the king showed compassion to the servant. Rather than selling off the servant, his family, and all he owed to repay the debt, the king freed the servant of his debt, canceling everything that he owed.

d) Explain how the servant, in turn, dealt with his fellow servant who owed him a hundred pence. What was the end result? (vv. 28-34)

The servant choked his fellow servant and demanded repayment. Though the fellow servant pleaded for patience, just as the servant had not long ago with the king, the servant showed no compassion and had his fellow servant thrown into prison. When word got back to the king, he sent for the servant, rebuked him for his lack of compassion and turned him over to the tormentors until his debt was repaid.

e) What is a condition of experiencing forgiveness from God? (v. 35)

In order to receive forgiveness from God, one must truly, from the heart, extend forgiveness to others.

3. Explain why this account is significant to us today. This biblical record illustrates that forgiveness is:

Based on God's Grace

Forgiveness is a divine act. By grace, God chooses to forgive us and no longer judge us for confessed sins.

A Movement from Bondage into Freedom

Before we confess our sins and are forgiven, we are in spiritual bondage, under sin's control. However, once God forgives our sin, we are free from sin's control.

Is Available to Everyone Who Truly Repents

God is willing to forgive *all* who come to Him. Jesus paid the price so that God can say, "you are forgiven."

4. Have the participants notice what forgiveness is **not**.

Forgiveness is Not Earned

We have done nothing, nor is there anything we can do, to earn forgiveness. Forgiveness is a *gift* from God. To receive this free gift, we confess our sins and repent.

Forgiveness is Not Forced or Coerced

Forgiveness is an act of free-will. It is an acknowledgment of a wrongdoing, but includes a willingness to let it go and a refusal to enact punishment for it. No one can be *made* to forgive someone.

Forgiveness is Not Contingent on Stipulations

True forgiveness is not saying, "I forgive you, but you must do . . . " True forgiveness does not require the performance of an action or a repayment of some sort by the person seeking forgiveness. God does not say, "You are forgiven, but first you must bear the following consequence." He simply forgives.

5. Finally, remind the participants that forgiveness is based on love. If we love others with the love of God—pure and unconditional—we will be more open to seek and give true forgiveness.

6. End the discussion by asking a volunteer to read Mark 2:1-12 aloud to the group.

C. CHAPTER HIGHLIGHTS

Using the content of Chapter Eight as background, give a general overview of the chapter. Be sure to include the following topics:

1. Forgiveness as a divine act of God
2. The necessity of forgiveness to our human condition
3. Through Jesus you *are* forgiven

PART TWO
A. BIBLE STUDY APPLICATION

1. Introduction

The Bible Study Application section contains eight questions which provide an opportunity to garner a deeper understanding of the meaning of forgiveness. The discussion of the Bible Study Application questions should confirm that the students understand the importance of Scripture.

Allow as much time as necessary to encourage the exchange of ideas and insights. Use the information preceding each set of questions to help introduce or close the discussion of a topic. Use the Bible verses to help keep the discussion on track. Depending on the size and personality of the group, you can discuss as many or as few of the questions as needed.

2. Procedure

Select Small Group Leaders. Ask for volunteers or select three small group leaders. Then assign each small group leader a number from 1-3. (This can also be done beforehand to save time.) Ask the small group leaders to write their numbers on large sheets of white paper so that they can be seen from a distance.

Divide into Small Groups. Inform the participants that they will be separated into small groups. Each group will study a different set of questions and then will present their findings to the larger group at the end of the study period. The questions should be assigned as follows:

> Group #1: The Meaning of Forgiveness
> Group #2: The Necessity of Forgiveness
> Group #3: The Certainty of Forgiveness

B. SMALL GROUP STUDY

1. Small Group Leaders

Each group will have one topic to explore. For each topic, there are questions and related Scripture references to stimulate discussion.

2. Sharing Insights

After 15 minutes, designate someone who will summarize the small group within the larger body of participants. Remind the designated person that she or he will only have five minutes to present.

3. Suggested Small Group Activity

If time permits, ask each group to complete the following activity to be presented when the entire class reconvenes: Each group is to cover a breaking news story for YAF-TV ("You Are Forgiven"). Using a passage from the Bible which illustrates forgiveness, for example the adulterous woman (John 8:2-11), Joseph forgiving his brothers (Genesis 46-47), have each member of the group play a role (news anchors, field reporters, actual participants) to report the events as they occurred. Just like a news broadcast, keep it tight. Give each group only 4 minutes.

C. LARGE GROUP PRESENTATIONS

Reconvene the Group. Call the small groups back together.

Explain the Procedure. Explain that a representative of each small group will share that group's reflections on the Bible Study Application questions with the larger group.

Remind Small Group Representatives of the time. Remind each group representative that he or she should try to summarize the group's discussion in five minutes. Allow up to five minutes to discuss each group's presentation. Afterwards, give each group four minutes to perform their skits.

D. LIFE APPLICATION DISCUSSION*

If time permits, the larger group can then discuss the Personal Application and Church Ministry questions together.

1. Introduction

The Personal Application sections contains four questions that encourage the participants to consider the teaching in light of their own lives. The Church Ministry Application section contains two questions which address some implications for the congregation as a whole.

2. Sharing Insights

This discussion should be open-ended and voluntary. The sharing of personal insights or recommendations for church ministry should be encouraged but not required. The group may have quite a bit to say. Watch the clock! Stop them after 10 minutes.

Answers are not provided for the Personal Application and Church Ministry sections because of the personal or specific nature of the questions.

E. PREPARATION FOR NEXT MEETING

Assignment. Have the participants read Chapter Nine, "Jesus Is More Than Enough" and review the questions in preparation for next week's session. Encourage them to come to the next session prepared to share their insights on the content of the chapter.

You may also want to assign small groups or particular questions to facilitate next week's meeting time.

F. CLOSING PRAYER

Form a circle, hold hands and ask for specific prayer requests. Then ask for several volunteers to pray, keeping the prayer requests in mind.

ANSWERS TO BIBLE STUDY APPLICATION
The Meaning of Forgiveness

True forgiveness comes from the very being of God. This was provided by God Himself in Christ Jesus for the sins of humanity.

1. Complete the following verses to understand how forgiveness is a gift of Divine grace.

a. Hebrews 9:14

How much more shall **the blood of Christ,** who through the eternal Spirit offered himself **without spot to God,** purge your conscience from dead works to serve the living God?

b. 2 Corinthians 5:21

For he hath **made him to be sin for us,** who knew no sin; that we **might be made the righteousness** of God in him.

c. Romans 3:25

Whom God hath set forth to be a **propitiation through faith** in his blood, to declare his righteousness for the **remission of sins** that are past, through the forbearance of God.

d. Acts 13:38

Be it known unto you therefore, men and brethren, that **through this man** is preached unto **you the forgiveness of sins.**

2. Read the following Scriptures and answer the questions.

a) Read Psalm 103:12. What does this Scripture tell us about God's forgiveness?

Answers will vary slightly. The east and west are infinitely apart; they will never meet. When God forgives us of our sins, He separates us from our sin and chooses never to judge us for them or associate us with them again.

b) Read Romans 3:20. What deed can one perform or what law should one obey to receive forgiveness?

By nature, man is sinful. Therefore, there is *no* human deed that a person can perform nor any human law one can obey to be justified in the sight of God. Forgiveness of sin comes only from God, through Jesus Christ (see also Hebrews 9:14).

3. Read John 8:2-11. What do these verses tell us about forgiveness?

These verses tell us that divine forgiveness is available freely to everyone who truly repents.

4. "And forgive us our debts, as we forgive our debtors" (Matthew 6:12). Use the following verses to answer questions about the extension of forgiveness to others.

a. Romans 12:17-21

How are you to live among men?
You are to live peacefully among men.
How are you to treat those who have done something "evil" to you?
You are not to return evil or try to avenge yourself. However, you should "overcome evil with good" and treat a person with kindness, leaving vengeance to God.

b. Ephesians 4:32
What are the three acts mentioned in this verse regarding treatment of others?
The three mentioned acts are kindness ("be ye kind"), tenderhearted, and forgiving.

c. Luke 17:3
What are you to do to your brother who trespasses against you?
You are to rebuke him.
If that same brother repents, what are you to do?
You are to forgive him.

d. Mark 11:25
What, according to this verse, are you to do for your brother while praying? How does this benefit you?
You are to forgive him. This benefits you because God forgives you when you forgive others.

The Necessity of Forgiveness
The Bible is clear that we as human beings are constantly living in opposition to God's righteousness and justice. We, by our very nature, are creatures in need of forgiveness.

5. Why is forgiveness necessary? Look up the following Scriptures and write the answers they give on the lines provided.
a. Psalm 51:5
Behold, I was shapen in iniquity; and in sin did my mother conceive me.
b. Romans 3:23
For all have sinned, and come short of the glory of God;
c. 1 John 1:8
If we say that we have no sin, we deceive ourselves, and the truth is not in us.

d. Choose one of the Scriptures above. What does it tell us about the necessity of forgiveness?

Answers will vary. Man is sinful by nature. Because Adam and Eve sinned (Genesis 3), every child born into the world was born a sinner and came into this world in need of salvation. If we don't admit that we are in need of forgiveness we are fooling ourselves. Though we may try to live "perfect" and "right" and "good" we are still sinners and it is not until we accept God's gift of forgiveness that we will be free of sin.

6. Even men of great biblical faith needed forgiveness. Match the following person with an act that necessitated forgiveness.

a. Moses (Numbers 20:1-13)   __c__ Allowed wives to turn his heart away from God

b. Peter (Matthew 26:69-75)   __d__ Had Uriah murdered

c. Solomon the Israelites (1 Kings 11:26-40)   __a__ Struck a rock to get water for

d. David (2 Samuel 11-12)   __b__ Denied Jesus

e. Jonah (Jonah 1)   __e__ Tried to avoid his call to Nineveh

The Certainty of Forgiveness

Jesus' death on the cross and resurrection *guaranteed* forgiveness. What a relief to know that all our sins are nailed to His cross.

7. Look at the following Scriptures. There are several errors in each one. Try to correct each Scripture without referring to your Bible.

a. **2 Chronicles 7:14**

"If my people, which are called by my name, shall **humble** themselves, and **pray**, and seek my **face**, and turn from their **wicked** ways; then will I hear from heaven, and will **forgive** their sin, and will heal their land.

b. **Luke 5:20**

And when he saw their **faith**, he said unto him, Man, **thy sins are forgiven thee.**

c. **John 1:29**

The next day John seeth **Jesus** coming unto him, and saith, Behold the **Lamb** of God, which **taketh away** the sin of the world.

d. **Romans 4:7**

Blessed are they whose **iniquities** are forgiven, and whose sins are **covered.**

8. Answer the following questions regarding the certainty of forgiveness.

a. Read Luke 23:39-43. Why did Jesus forgive the criminal moments before his death?

Jesus forgave the criminal because the criminal truly repented and acknowledged Jesus as the Saviour. While the other criminal being crucified mocked Jesus and hurled insults at Him, this criminal sought forgiveness and asked Jesus to remember him when Jesus came into His kingdom. It is never to late to ask for forgiveness.

b. Read John 8:2-11. How did Jesus handle those who wanted to stone the adulterous woman?

Jesus offered a challenge: whoever was without sin should be the first one to throw a stone. This played on their conscious. Each person was a sinner. How could they possibly stone a woman for her sin when each was guilty of sin of their own? The group disassembled; no one had stoned her. Jesus asked the woman if anyone had condemned her for her sin. She replied, "no." Jesus replied that He would not condemn her either.

LIFE APPLICATION
Personal Application

1. When do you think you should forgive someone: before or after they have confessed?

2. Does God keep count of the number of times He forgives us? (Jeremiah 31:33-34)

3. With the response from number two in mind, answer the following:
Should you keep track of the number of times you forgive someone?
Should you put a limit on forgiveness?

What might happen if you keep count of the number of times you have extended forgiveness to others?

4. If you know that someone has yet to forgive another, should you refuse to forgive that person?

Church Ministry Application

1. Many people refuse or are afraid to turn to God because they feel that they've lived so horribly and committed such terrible deeds that even God can't forgive them. What is the responsibility of the church in regard to these people? Is it the church's duty to intercede for these people?

2. In today's frantically paced world, people have less and less patience and are seemingly more prone and quick to anger. How can the church continue to stress the importance of forgiveness in such a climate?

SESSION NINE

JESUS IS MORE THAN ENOUGH

For sessions of 90 minutes or more, use the lesson format for PART ONE and PART TWO.

PART ONE

ACTIVITY	TIME
Opening Prayer	5 minutes
Scripture Search	20 minutes
Chapter Highlights	20 minutes

PART TWO

ACTIVITY	TIME
Small Group Study	15 minutes
Large Group Presentations	27 minutes
Life Application Discussion	10 minutes
Closing Prayer	3 minutes

For sessions of less than 90 minutes, use PART ONE only and assign the Bible Study Application questions as homework.

Lesson Aims: By the end of the lesson, students will: a) explore how Jesus met the multitude's need for food; b) become convinced of God's knowledge of and ability to supply their needs; and c) determine to trust God to keep His promises to supply their needs.

PART ONE
A. OPENING PRAYER

Open the session with prayer. Include the requests that God would help each participant to:

Understand that God knows our needs and has more than adequate means to provide them.

Realize that they can ask God for what they need.

Trust that God will supply their needs and much more.

B. SCRIPTURE SEARCH

1. Ask someone to read Mark 6:30 aloud to the group.

2. Use the following questions

to review the facts from this Scripture passage:

a) When the disciples returned from their tours, what did they do? (v. 30)

When they returned from their missions, they sought out Jesus so they could tell Him what they did and taught while on their missions.

b) What was Jesus' suggestion to them? (v. 31)

Jesus realized they were tired and He suggested that they go to a desert place where they could rest.

c) What was Jesus' attitude toward the crowd who had followed Him? (v. 34) Jesus was moved with compassion.

d) Why did the disciples want to send the crowds away? (v. 36)

The disciples wanted to send the crowds away because they had nothing to eat. They wanted them to go into the countries and villages and get themselves some food.

e) How much food was readily available for Jesus, the apostles, and the crowd? (v. 38) There was five loaves of bread and two fish.

f) How did Jesus tell the apostles to divide the people? (v. 40)

They were divided into groups of hundreds and fifties.

g) What did Jesus do with the food He had available? (v. 41)

Jesus took the available food, blessed it, and gave it to the disciples to distribute among the people. The five loaves of bread and two fish was divided among everyone!

h) How much was each person given? Just enough to sustain them? (v. 42) Each person was given enough not only to sustain them, but to fill (satisfy) them.

i) After everyone had eaten, was there any food remaining? (v. 43)

There was twelve baskets full remaining.

j) According to Scripture, how many men were fed from the original five loaves of bread and two fish? (v. 44)
Five thousand!

3. Ask the group to differentiate between a need and a desire. Allow a few minutes for volunteer response. A "need," as defined in the dictionary, is a lack of something required. A "desire," as defined in the dictionary, is a longing, a craving, a want. Explain that desires:
- Tend to be selfish (Judges 9:2-5)
- Can become obsessive (Numbers 11:4-6)
- Can cause an internal battle between flesh and spirit (Galatians 5:17)
- May be sinful (Galatians 5:24-26)
- Can lead to fighting and disagreements (James 4:2)

4. Finally, point out to the group that having needs of our own does not exempt us from tending to the needs of others (2 Kings 6:1-7; Matthew 23:1-12; Luke 6:35).

5. End the discussion by asking a volunteer to read Mark 8:14-21 aloud to the group.

C. CHAPTER HIGHLIGHTS

Using the content of Chapter Nine as background, give a general overview of the chapter. Be sure to include the following topics:
1. The Miracle—The Feeding of the Five Thousand
2. The Message of the Miracle
3. The Application of the Miracle Truth

PART TWO
A. BIBLE STUDY APPLICATION
1. Introduction

The Bible Study Application section contains nine questions which provide an opportunity to garner a deeper understanding that God is more than enough to meet all of our needs. The discussion of the Bible Study Application questions should confirm that the students understand the importance of Scripture.

Allow as much time as necessary to encourage the exchange of ideas and insights. Use the information preceding each set of questions to help introduce or close the discussion of a topic. Use the Bible verses to help keep the discussion on track. Depending on the size and personality of the group, you can discuss as many or as few of the questions as needed.

2. Procedure

Select Small Group Leaders. Ask for volunteers or select three small group leaders. Then assign each small group leader a number from 1-3. (This can also be done beforehand to save time.) Ask the small group leaders to write their numbers on large sheets of white paper so that they can be seen from a distance.

Divide into Small Groups. Inform the participants that they will be separated into small groups. Each group will study a different set of questions and then will present their findings to the larger group at the end of the study period. The questions should be assigned as follows:

Group #1: The Determination of Our Needs (questions #1-4)

Group #2: The Supply of Our Needs (questions #5-7)
Group #3: The Overflowing Abundance for Our Needs (questions #8-9)

B. SMALL GROUP STUDY

1. Small Group Leaders

Each group will have one topic to explore. For each topic, there are questions and related Scripture references to stimulate discussion.

2. Sharing Insights

After 15 minutes, designate someone who will summarize the small group within the larger body of participants. Remind the designated person that she or he will only have five minutes to present.

3. Suggested Group Activity

After the class divides into groups, give the leader of each group either a large cup, a bowl, or a clean household cleaner bottle. Each group should have a different item. Show each group a soup ladle and ask the group to guess how many dips of the ladle are needed to completely fill their item with water. When the large group reconvenes, allow one person to fill the item with the guessed ladle amount. How close were their guesses? Were some over? Were some close, but just not enough? Ask them to discuss how this illustrates God's knowledge of and meeting of our needs.

C. LARGE GROUP PRESENTATIONS

Reconvene the Group. Call the small groups back together.

Explain the Procedure. Explain that a representative of each small group will share that group's reflections on the Bible Study Application questions with the larger group.

Remind Small Group Representatives of the time. Remind each group representative that he or she should try to summarize the group's discussion in five minutes. Allow up to five minutes to discuss each group's presentation.

D. LIFE APPLICATION DISCUSSION*

If time permits, the larger group can then discuss the Personal Application and Church Ministry questions together.

1. Introduction

The Personal Application sections contains three questions that encourage the participants to consider the teaching in light of their own lives. The Church Ministry Application section contains two questions which address some implications for the congregation as a whole.

2. Sharing Insights

This discussion should be open-ended and voluntary. The sharing of personal insights or recommendations for church ministry should be encouraged but not required. The group may have quite a bit to say. Watch the clock! Stop them after 10 minutes.

Answers are not provided for the Personal Application and Church Ministry sections because of the personal or specific nature of the questions.

E. PREPARATION FOR NEXT MEETING

Assignment. Have the participants read Chapter Ten, "Jesus Is the Light of the World" and review the questions in preparation for next week's session. Encourage them to come to the next session prepared to share their insights on the content of the chapter.

You may also want to assign small groups or particular questions to facilitate next week's meeting time.

F. CLOSING PRAYER

Form a circle, hold hands and ask for specific prayer requests. Then ask for several volunteers to pray, keeping the prayer requests in mind.

ANSWERS TO BIBLE STUDY APPLICATION

The Determination of Our Needs

God is the source of supply for all the needs of those who trust in Divine providence. When making an appeal to God to meet a need that we have, first we must determine exactly *what our need is,* and not confuse it with a desire. Fortunately for us, God already knows them!

1. Read the following Scriptures that prove that God knows our needs.

a. John 5:5-9

How long was the man said to be infirmed? (v. 5)

Thirty eight years.

Did Jesus already know what was wrong with the man?

Verse six says, "Jesus saw him and *knew* that he had been now a long time in that case.

b. Proverbs 15:3
How can God be aware of the needs of everyone all at the same time?
The eyes of the Lord are in every place—He is with us all the time, therefore none of our needs escape Him.

2. Unscramble the following verse from Matthew 6:11
"GIVE US THIS DAY OUR DAILY BREAD"
Why is this Scripture important when considering your needs?
Answers will vary. Matthew 6:11 challenges us to focus on our current needs, not those we anticipate. It calls on us to trust that our needs will be provided exactly when they need to be. In addition, it helps us to learn to be patient and to wait on God (see also Psalms 37:7).

3. Even though God knows all of our needs, He still wants us to bring them to Him. Match the following Scriptures with their references.

c—**Genesis 18:32**
"And he said, Oh let not the Lord be angry, and I will speak yet but this once: Peradventure ten shall be found there. And he said, I will not destroy it for ten's sake."

a—**Genesis 25:21**
"And Isaac intreated the Lord for his wife, because she was barren: and the Lord was intreated of him, and Rebekah his wife conceived."

b—**James 4:2**
"Ye lust, and have not: ye kill, and desire to have, and cannot obtain: ye fight and war, yet ye have not, because ye ask not."

e—**Matthew 21:22**
"And all things, whatsoever ye shall ask in prayer, believing, ye shall receive."

d—**James 1:5-6**
"If any of you lack wisdom, let him ask of God, that giveth to all men liberally, and upbraideth not; and it shall be given him. But let him ask in faith, nothing wavering."

4. Can we truly ask God for anything? Read Mark 10:35-40. What did James and John ask for? What was Jesus' response?
James and John asked Jesus to let them sit on either side of Him in glory (v. 37). Jesus denied their request, but did not mock or scold them for asking (vv. 39-40). Sometimes our requests will be met with a "no" but that should not deter us from asking.

The Supply of Our Needs
"Now to Abraham and his seed were the promises made." Galatians 3:16

God promised that the needs of those who trust in Him will be met.

5. Complete each verse that speaks of God's promises.

Psalm 23:5

"Thou preparest a table before me in the presence of mine enemies: thou anointest my head with oil; **my cup runneth over.**"

Psalm 37:3

"Trust in the Lord, and do good; so shalt thou dwell in the land, and verily **thou shalt be fed.**"

Matthew 6:33

But seek ye first the kingdom of God, and his righteousness; and **all these things shall be added unto you.**"

Philippians 4:19

"But my God shall **supply all your need** according to his riches in glory by Christ Jesus."

Psalm 9:18

"For the **needy shall not alway be forgotten:** the expectation of the poor shall not perish for ever."

6. God also made promises about our meeting the needs of others. Complete each verse that speaks on these promises.

Mark 10:21

"Then Jesus beholding him loved him, and said unto him, One thing thou lackest: go thy way, sell whatsoever thou hast, and give to the poor, and **thou shalt have treasure in heaven:** and come, take up the cross, and follow me."

Luke 6:35

"But love ye your enemies, and do good, and **lend, hoping for nothing again; and your reward shall be great,** and ye shall be the children of the Highest: for he is kind unto the unthankful and to the evil."

7. Deuteronomy 6:11-12, warns, "When thou shalt have eaten and be full; Then beware lest thou forget the Lord." The following Biblical figures were "full" and "forgot" the Lord. Match each person to his description.

c Had everything. Lived in Paradise. Allowed Satan to tempt Him.

a Survived the flood, but got drunk and cursed his Son, Ham.

b Prosperous and successful. Committed adultery and murder.

d Wisest man on earth, wealthy, powerful, yet allowed his wives to turn his heart from God.

a. Noah; b. David; c. David; d. Solomon

The Overflowing Abundance of Our Needs

Sometimes Jesus Christ does not supply just enough, He can provide far more than we'd ever need.

8. Look up the Scriptures to answer the questions below.

a. Read Ephesians 3:20. What does it say about God's ability to provide?

It says, God "is able to do exceeding abundantly above all that we ask or think."

b. Read 1 Kings 17:10-16. How did God provide for the widow?

The widow had very little, but God commanded Elijah the prophet to go to her and she would feed him. Though she only had a "handful of meal and a little oil," God promised, if she did as instructed, that the "meal wouldn't waste" or "oil fail" until "rain came upon the earth." He would take care of her. And He did just that. Scripture tells us that the widow and her house ate for *many* days.

c. "It is a good thing to give thanks unto the Lord, and to sing praises unto thy name, O most High" (Psalm 92:1). In order to remain thankful for all of the needs God has supplied, it is important to avoid focusing our thoughts on the things that we don't have. How can we do that?

9. Find the following Scriptures and write them below.

Exodus 20:17

"Thou shalt not covet thy neighbour's house, thou shalt not covet thy neighbour's wife, nor his manservant, nor his maidservant, nor his ox, nor his ass, nor any thing that is thy neighbour's."

Acts 20:33

"I have coveted no man's silver, or gold, or apparel."

Philippians 4:11

"Not that I speak in respect of want: for I have learned, in whatsoever state I am, therewith to be content."

1 Thessalonians 5:18

"In every thing give thanks: for this is the will of God in Christ Jesus concerning you."

LIFE APPLICATION

Personal Application

1. "Ye have not, because ye ask not" (James 4:2). Have you asked God to supply your needs? Has He ever responded by giving *more* than you requested?

2. Think back to the definition of a "desire" and a "need." Have you ever

prayed for a selfish desire and mistaken it for a need? What was the outcome?

3. How does seeking "first the kingdom of God" (Matthew 6:33) help when you are faced with an urgent need?

Church Ministry Application

1. How can the church demonstrate through action that God supplies the needs of His people?

2. Are church members who are considerably "well off" more responsible for meeting the needs of others?

SESSION TEN
JESUS IS THE LIGHT OF THE WORLD

For sessions of 90 minutes or more, use the lesson format for PART ONE and PART TWO.

PART ONE

ACTIVITY	TIME
Introduction and Opening Prayer	5 minutes
Scripture Search	20 minutes
Chapter Highlights	15 minutes

PART TWO

ACTIVITY	TIME
Bible Study Application	20 minutes
Answers to Bible Study Application	20 minutes
Life Application Discussion	10 minutes

For sessions of less than 90 minutes, use PART ONE only and assign the Bible Study Application questions as home

Lesson Aims: At the end of this two-part Bible study session, the participants should be able to: a) understand the significance of Jesus opening the eyes of the man born blind; b) recognize the value of spiritual light; and c) be convinced of their need to become light bearers to those who need to know Him who is the Light of the World.

A. INTRODUCTION

Begin by writing today's topic on the chalkboard, and then draw an imaginary line through your class. Ask the students on one side to name some of the benefits of light. They may mention that light promotes growth, it helps us to see clearly, it purifies, it shows us the direction to take, it cheers us, it shows us what is right, and so forth. As each benefit of light is mentioned, ask the other side to tell how that characteristic is true of Jesus. For instance, just as light promotes growth, Jesus, the Light of the World, causes spiritual growth in those close to Him. Just as light enables us to see clearly, Jesus is the One who helps us to clearly discern spiritual truth. And so on.

Finish this activity by telling the class that they will investigate the situation in which Jesus told His disciples that He was and is the Light of the World.

A. OPENING PRAYER

Open the session with prayer. Include the requests that God would help participants to:

- Recognize their own areas of spiritual blindness.
- Develop compassion toward those with physical limitations.
- Witness to those in spiritual darkness.

C. SCRIPTURE SEARCH

1. Begin by asking one student to read John 9:1-11. Ask another to read John 9:35-41.

2. Jesus is revealed in the Gospel of John through some very strong, metaphorical statements made by the Lord, Himself. Before class begins, give six students slips of paper with the following references: John 6:35; John 8:12; John 10:11; John 11:25; John 14:6; and John 15:1. Ask each one to stand and read his or her assigned verse. These verses tell us that Jesus is the Bread of Life, the Light of the World, the Good Shepherd, the Resurrection and the Life, the Way, the Truth, and the Vine. "Why do you think Jesus made these statements?" Metaphors that allow us to gain insight that might not be apparent otherwise. Some of these statements were made in the midst of incidents which illustrated the aspects of Jesus' personality which were used as metaphors. Today's passage includes one of the "I am..." statements and happens in the context of Jesus healing both spiritual blindness and physical blindness.

D. CHAPTER HIGHLIGHTS

Before discussing the chapter, review the following term:

Pharisees—the religious leaders who taught other Jews how to obey Scripture. Their interpretations were very legalistic, and often they themselves did not obey the rules they made. They were very jealous of Jesus because the people's honor seemed to be going to Him instead of them. Although they studied the details of Old Testament Law, they often missed the broad principles of Scripture, such as love for one another.

Using the content of Chapter Ten as background, give a general overview of the chapter. Be sure to include the following topics:
1. The biblical attitude toward physical disabilities.
2. Understanding our own difficulties in life.
3. The journey of the man born blind from spiritual blindness to light.
4. The reason Jesus identified Himself as the Light of the World.

PART TWO
A. BIBLE STUDY APPLICATION
1. Introduction

By this time students should be adept in inductive Bible studies (as this one is). A number of Bible discussion leaders should have been developed. Encourage students to start home Bible studies using this method. (Urban Ministries, Inc. has many additional Bible study books, which may be used in a variety of settings.)

2. Procedure

Choose leaders from among those who have studied their lessons and filled in the answers. The ideal size of a small group is somewhere between five and fifteen. Encourage the leaders to stay within the time constraints and cover all the material. Continue to develop good leaders. Good leaders try to draw everyone into the discussion. When they notice someone not participating, they may try to call them by name and ask them to give an answer to an easier question. Discussions are a good way of learning, because: We remember some of what we hear, more of what we read, but most of what we ourselves are involved in doing. Discussion is one of the first steps in active learning.

C. ANSWERS TO BIBLE STUDY APPLICATION

As the following three questions are discussed, guide students toward looking at Jesus compassion for human needs, as well as His teaching of spiritual truths.

Jesus Is the Light of the World (John 9:1-5)

As Jesus left the temple, He stopped by one of the many who hung around near the temple hoping that some temple-goers would give them some alms (money for the poor). Jesus had lessons for His disciples as well as two wonderful gifts for a blind person. Read John 9:1-5.

1. Attitudes toward disabilities have undergone some changes since bib-

lical days. What reasons did the disciples suspect were the causes of physical challenges? Do people have some of the same attitudes today? Should we be able to tell the cause of a disability? What do you think Jesus was teaching His disciples in the first three verses? What should be our attitude toward disabilities? What can we learn regarding our own trials?

False religious leaders may perform amazing "miracles," but Jesus' miracles were more than spectacular tricks. His miracles showed His Deity and they showed His love for people. Many of His miracles involved helping people with disabilities. People tend to look for someone to blame for trouble of any kind. Often they blame the victim. Even though the book of Job demonstrates that human suffering can be the result of spiritual battles that humans are unaware of, people continue to show little sympathy for people in need.

2. Jesus healed many diseases and disabilities, but none more often than blindness. What is one important teaching Jesus wanted to convey through this type of miracle? (v. 5)

Jesus came to heal spiritual blindness as well as physical blindness. He came to bring spiritual light as well as healing of spiritual darkness.

3. The "I" beginning verse 4 is more properly translated "we." What important principle is Jesus setting forth regarding our work on earth? What is He teaching us regarding our use of time?

Just as Jesus was aware that His time for ministry on earth was limited, so should we. We should use our time wisely for the work of the Kingdom.

Jesus Gives Sight to the Blind Man (John 9:6-11)

Help students to see the human interaction as you discuss the answers to the following questions.

4. Look at verses 6 and 7 to see the method Jesus used in this healing. How did this healing differ from other instances of Christ's healing people? What did this method require of the blind man? What do you suppose he was thinking as he walked to the pool of Siloam? In your own experience, does Jesus ever require steps of faith that do not seem logical to us? Jesus used a physical means of healing the man that might be compared to a medication of some sort. What part does medicine play in everyday healing?

As Jesus healed people of various diseases and disabilities, He used a variety of approaches. Sometimes He spoke, other times He touched, and in this case, He used mud. People have made many conjectures as to why Jesus used this method. All we can say for sure is that Jesus used a variety of approaches for a variety of people in a variety of circumstances.

Point out to students, if no one else does, that the practice of medicine uses an understanding that God gives regarding how our bodies and other substances of His creation can interact for our good. God often uses humanity's understanding of medication and other medical processes to heal our bodies.

5. Imagine the response of the formerly blind man's neighbors. Why do you think they responded as they did? How would you feel if you saw a person who had been born blind now seeing clearly? What would you do?

Stop for a quick role-play set in a contemporary community. Choose someone to be a blind beggar. Choose others to be neighbors. Act out an encounter with the blind man with his neighbors on that first day of his healing. Include his surprise at seeing what they look like and their reactions to him.

6. Read the responses of the blind man in John 9:11-12, 17, 25-27, 30-33, 35-38 and note the formerly blind man's growing understanding of who Jesus is. How would you describe his spiritual understanding in each of these stages? What things helped him to grow in his understanding of who Jesus is?

In the first two verses listed, the formerly blind man only knew Jesus by His name. All he knew was that Jesus healed him. As the Pharisees questioned him some more, he reflected more on what Jesus had done and he called Him a prophet. Then the Pharisees called him back a third time. As he recounted the healing again, he acknowledged that those who listen to Jesus are His disciples. The Pharisees continued questioning him and he reasoned that Jesus could not be a sinner, because God answered the prayers of Jesus in a wonderful way. Therefore he proclaimed that Jesus must be of God. When his faith journey took the formerly blind man to such a conclusion, the Pharisees threw him out of the temple. Then Jesus found the man again and asked him if he believed on the Son of God. He said he was ready to believe if he just knew who the Son of God was. When Jesus identified Himself as the Son of God, the formerly blind man said, "Lord, I believe," and he worshiped Him.

This man grew in spiritual understanding through experiencing a miracle by Jesus, through his own reasoning energized by and in spite of the intimidation of unbelievers, and through the words of Jesus Himself. Point out to your students that we all have different paths that lead us to knowing and trusting in Jesus, but the coming to Him in faith is the same end result. Just as the formerly blind man came to Christ through a gradual recognition of who Jesus is, most of us go through a period of progressive understanding, whether it is one day or many.

Jesus Defines Sight (John 9:35-41)

By the time we get to John 9:35-41, the formerly blind man has been excommunicated from the synagogue for stating his conclusion that Jesus came from God. He has gone from physical blindness to seeing and is now on the verge of going from spiritual blindness to spiritual sight.

As you discuss the following questions, note how Jesus brings the conversation around from the issue of the specific miracle to the greater questions that confront all of us.

7. With what question does Jesus confront the formerly blind man? Why do you think Jesus sought him out again? What is the response of the man? Imagine the thoughts that may be going through his mind as he asks Jesus to tell who the Son of Man is. What does he say is his motivation in wanting to know who the Son of Man is?

Jesus asked the formerly blind man if he believed on the Son of God. Jesus undoubtedly wanted the man to make a decision as to who Jesus is and to make a commitment to Him. Maybe the man was beginning to see who Jesus was as he asked his question, but he wanted to be sure he had the right answer.

8. What is the formerly blind man's response to Jesus' revelation of who He is? Note his action as well as his verbal response. What things led him to this conclusion?

Not only did the man tell Jesus that he believed on Him as the Son of God, he also worshiped Him as Lord. Several things had led his to this conclusion. He had been blessed in being healed and then he began reasoning out the answers to spiritual questions. But the final push was Jesus' statement of who He was.

9. When the man expressed his belief and commitment, Jesus made a statement that was obviously overheard. Who else was listening to Jesus? Why do you think they were listening? Write in your own words the meaning of Jesus' statement in verse 39.

Jesus said that He came to bring light to the blind and to bring judgment on those who were able to see physically, but not spiritually. The Pharisees were probably listening because they wanted to trap Jesus by His own words as well as the things He was doing.

10. Do you think the Pharisees understood Jesus' statement in verse 39? What was their response? What does this show about their spiritual state?

How does such an attitude keep people from coming to true spiritual light?

The Pharisees understood that Jesus was calling them spiritually blind, and they could not believe that was true of them. Knowing our own spiritual need is necessary to finding the light.

LIFE APPLICATION
Personal Application
Jesus Is the Light of My Life

Some of the questions for today's personal application *are* very personal. If students have not filled out this section in advance, read through the questions and allow some time for quiet reflection. Then individuals may volunteer answers as to how this course has changed their perspectives of who Jesus is, and how it has changed their hearts and lives.

1. How is Jesus the light of *your* life? The man born blind said to Jesus, "I believe." Have you put your trust in Jesus as Saviour? Have you been saved (born again)? Then the formerly blind man worshiped the Lord Jesus. This is a change in attitude or feelings. Such a change affects our hearts and emotions. Have you come to the place where you have made Jesus the ruler of your life? What differences should you see as a result of this step of commitment?

2. Over a very short time the man born blind had a gradual increase in his understanding of who Jesus is. Describe new perspectives you may have realized over this short ten session course regarding Jesus, the Light of the World. The formerly blind man put his trust in Jesus as Saviour and Lord. How has your relationship with Christ changed as a result of this course?

3. Just as the sun is the light of our universe, so Jesus is the spiritual light of our world. The moon is a reflection of the sun, and we, as Christians, are meant to reflect the light of Christ. How is your life reflecting Jesus Christ?

Church Ministry Application
Jesus Is the Light of Our Church

This section is meant to summarize the things learned as church ministry application. Start a new program or become involved in an old church program in a way that energizes and revitalizes that program in order to apply the truths learned and continue fellowship established in this course. Participating in a community witnessing program, a homeless shelter, an active food pantry, a tutoring program or a neighborhood Bible study are just a few ideas for the implementation of this section.

1. Is your church reflecting the Light of the World? Your church may be

surrounded with much darkness and so the church is needed all the more to bring the Light. How is your church bringing light into your community?

2. What is your part in the ministry of your church? Are you involved in the work your church is doing?

3. Is there a special project that this class can begin? Do more than just suggest plans. Start a project and stay with it. Let this project be a memorial to the things learned at this time and the community developed within the class.

NOTES